The Cold War
1945–1989

Simon Wood

HODDER
GIBSON
AN HACHETTE UK COMPANY

The Publishers would like to thank the following for permission to reproduce copyright material:

Photo credits: sidebar image p.1–109 © tribalium123 – 123RF; p.2 © Photos.com – Thinkstock/Getty Images; p.4 © MARKA / Alamy Stock Photo; p.5 © Allan Jackson/Hulton Archive/Getty Images; p.6 (top) © David Cole / Alamy Stock Photo, (middle) © AFP/AFP/Getty Images, (bottom)© Paul Popper/Popperfoto/Getty Images; p.9 © GL Archive / Alamy Stock Photo; p.11 'Peep under the Iron curtain' - Illingworth, Daily Mail, 6 March 1946 © Associated Newspapers Ltd. / Solo Syndication (National Library of Wales, Aberystwyth) p.15 © Alphathon via Wikipedia (https://creativecommons.org/licenses/by-sa/3.0/deed.en); p.26 © FPG/Archive Photos/Getty Images; p.30 © Al Fenn/The LIFE Picture Collection/Getty Images; p.33 © Keystone-France/Gamma-Keystone via Getty Images; p.34 © Sovfoto/UIG via Getty Images; p.38 © Keystone-France/Gamma-Keystone via Getty Images; p.39 © Wolfgang Bera/ullstein bild via Getty Images; p.45 © GL Archive / Alamy Stock Photo; p.50 © Bettmann – Getty Images; p.53 © NY Daily News Archive via Getty Images; p.55 © The Estate of Karl Hubenthal in the publication; p.61 © Popperfoto/Getty Images; p.63 © Keystone-France/Gamma-Keystone via Getty Images; p.66 © Bettmann – Getty Images; p.69 © Keystone-France\Gamma-Rapho via Getty Images; p.71 © Bettmann – Getty Images; p.72 © John Filo/Getty Images; p.74 © AFP/AFP/Getty Images; p.82 'OK Mr President, let's talk', Illingworth - Daily Mail 29 October 1962 © Solo Syndication (National Library of Wales) p.84 © Nicholas Garland via The Kent University Cartoon Archive p.90 © Central Press/Getty Images; p.95 © Harry Langdon/Getty Images; p.97 © Robert Nickelsberg/The LIFE Images Collection/Getty Images; p.99 (top) © Wojtek Laski/East News/Getty Images, (bottom) © Probst/ullstein bild via Getty Images; p.101 © Georges De Keerle/Getty Images; p.104 © Topfoto/Keystone.

Every effort has been made to trace all copyright holders, but if any have been inadvertently overlooked the Publishers will be pleased to make the necessary arrangements at the first opportunity.

Although every effort has been made to ensure that website addresses are correct at time of going to press, Hodder Gibson cannot be held responsible for the content of any website mentioned in this book. It is sometimes possible to find a relocated web page by typing in the address of the home page for a website in the URL window of your browser.

Hachette UK's policy is to use papers that are natural, renewable and recyclable products and made from wood grown in sustainable forests. The logging and manufacturing processes are expected to conform to the environmental regulations of the country of origin.

Orders: please contact Bookpoint Ltd, 130 Milton Park, Abingdon, Oxon OX14 4SB. Telephone: (44) 01235 827720. Fax: (44) 01235 400454. Lines are open 9.00–5.00, Monday to Saturday, with a 24-hour message answering service. Visit our website at www.hoddereducation.co.uk. Hodder Gibson can be contacted direct on: Tel: 0141 848 1609; Fax: 0141 889 6315; email: hoddergibson@hodder.co.uk

© Simon Wood 2016

First published in 2016 by
Hodder Gibson, an imprint of Hodder Education,
An Hachette UK Company
2a Christie Street
Paisley PA1 1NB

Impression number 5 4 3 2 1
Year   2020 2019 2018 2017 2016

Cover photo © yuri 4u80 – Fotolia; © brizz666 – Fotolia (insert)
Illustrations by Aptara, Inc.
Typeset in India by Aptara, Inc.
Printed in Slovenia

A catalogue record for this title is available from the British Library
ISBN: 978 14718 5250 3

Contents

Introduction

What is this book about?

This book is about the Cold War. The Cold War is the term given to the period of history from the end of the Second World War in 1945 to the collapse of communism in Eastern Europe in the late 1980s. It was a time of competition between two blocs of countries. On one side were the Western democracies, led by the United States of America. The other bloc was dominated by communist Russia and was made up of the Soviet Union or USSR (United Soviet Socialist Republics) and her satellite states in Eastern Europe. The Soviet Union was made up of a number of republics, of which Russia was only one part. For example, modern day Ukraine and the Baltic states were part of the Soviet Union until it broke up. Both America and the Soviet Union were known as superpowers as both controlled large military forces and were the dominant powers within their power blocs.

This conflict is called the Cold War because no active fighting, or 'hot war', took place between the United States and the Soviet Union. In fact fighting did take place between those who supported communism and those who supported the Western democracies. These wars even included American and Soviet forces at times. However, American and Soviet ground troops never actually faced each other in combat. Conflicts that occurred during the Cold War include the Korean War (1950–53), the Vietnam War (1964–75) and the Soviet–Afghan War (1979–89). Thus, despite a breakdown of relations between the superpowers a direct hot war between both sides was actually avoided – just.

At the heart of the Cold War lay differences in the ideology of both sides. The simplest definition of ideology is a system of beliefs and ideas that form the basis of a political system. Broadly, the Americans supported capitalism and the Soviets supported communism. Both sides also developed military alliances and spent massively on armaments, especially nuclear arms, in order to make the other side think very carefully about the risks of attacking them. At times the world came dangerously close to nuclear war, such as during the Cuban Missile Crisis of 1962. This near miss led to talks between the two sides and attempts to control the arms race. In the end, the pressures of a failing economy, changing leadership and a restless population led to the collapse of communism in Eastern Europe. At the time, this sudden collapse of communism came as a great surprise to most people.

How will this book help you?

This book will help you to be successful in your Higher History course. It contains everything you need to know about the unit called 'The Cold War, 1945–89'. The Higher History course is developed through understanding six issues. These issues are the areas for which extended responses are needed. In any year, three of the six areas will be sampled by the SQA. This means that you should study at least four of the six issues so that you are able to answer at least one question. Your teacher or lecturer will make sure you have a choice in the final examination.

The activities

At the end of each chapter, there are three parts to help you prepare for the exam:

1 The first part, 'Activities', is designed to help you make use of the information in the chapter, organise it and develop some notes in a variety of ways.

2 The second part, 'Unit assessment practice,' is an example of a unit assessment type task. All unit assessments will be organised by your centre. The unit assessment is designed to show a minimum competence in the topic in terms of skills and knowledge. You may use this as a practice question.

3 The third part, 'Extended response practice and Top Tip,' provides advice as to successfully completing the extended response in your exam. Each has a useful tip and an extended response question for you to practise with, should you wish.

1 Why did the Cold War emerge in the years up to 1955?

The Second World War (1939–45) was fought to destroy Nazi Germany. This fight had led to an alliance between Great Britain, the Soviet Union and the United States of America to defeat the common enemy of Nazi Germany. However, the allies did not trust each other at all. Once the war ended in 1945, old misunderstandings between America and Britain on one side and the Soviet Union on the other soon emerged. The basis of this was the mistrust each side had for the other's ideology.

The impact of the First World War and the Russian Revolution

The origins of this distrust go back to events during the First World War (1914–18). The First World War was fought between Britain, France, Russia and America on one side, and Germany, Austria-Hungary and the Turkish Empire on the other side.

In 1917 Russia withdrew from the First World War and in March 1918 made peace with Germany. Russia had fought Germany for three years and was exhausted by war. Russia was ruled by a monarchy in the years up to 1917, and the ruler was known as the Tsar (or Emperor) of Russia. However, early in 1917 Russia's population rose up against the ruling Tsarist dynasty and in February 1917 Tsar Nicholas II was forced to abdicate. Although a provisional government was formed and tried to continue fighting in the war, it was in turn overthrown by a revolutionary group, known as the Bolsheviks, in October 1917. The Bolsheviks were led by Vladimir Ilyich Ulyanov, who was known as Lenin. Lenin was a communist. He followed the ideas of Karl Marx and thought that these ideas would allow Russia to prosper and become a more equal society.

The events of the First World War gave the Bolsheviks an opportunity to seize power. The war did not go well for the Russians. Their army performed poorly against the Germans and when the Tsar took over leadership of the army, he became associated with military defeats. Nicholas was not a strong or decisive man and his authority within Russia eventually collapsed. When he was faced with the reality that neither the army nor the population supported him, Nicholas abdicated, or stood down from, the throne. In October 1917 the Bolsheviks seized power. Facing many enemies

within Russia, the Bolsheviks negotiated a peace with Germany, called the Treaty of Brest-Litovsk. In reality, the Treaty was a victory for the Germans, who imposed terms on the communists, but it did give the Bolsheviks the breathing space needed to defeat their internal enemies, called the 'Whites'.

Source 1.1

Vladimir Ilyich Ulyanov, known as Lenin (1870–1924): Russian communist and leader of the 1917 Bolshevik Revolution. He died in 1924 after a series of strokes.

Politicians in the Western democracies did not give the new Bolshevik Government much chance of survival. Despite this, the Government did survive and the Russian peace treaty with Germany allowed the transfer of significant numbers of German troops away from the East to fight in the West. Lenin also had no intention of paying back the debts of money that the old Tsarist regime had run up fighting the war. Much of this money had been borrowed from countries like Great Britain.

Following the peace treaty, the Bolsheviks set about creating the world's first socialist state. Lenin and his fellow Bolsheviks aimed to create a country where there was equality for all. There would be common ownership of land and industry, decent education and free healthcare. In reality, in order to survive, the new Union of Soviet Socialist Republics (USSR) became a totalitarian state. There was a secret police (the 'Cheka', which would eventually became the infamous KGB) to deal with those who were anti-revolutionary. Only one political party, the Communist Party, was allowed. Land and industry were taken over by the government and run, in theory, for the benefit of all. The economy was planned by the government; no private enterprise was allowed.

The Western allies were horrified. Initially, the withdrawal of Russia from the war unleashed a huge German offensive on the American, British and French armies on the Western Front. However, the German offensive ran out of momentum and the allies launched a decisive counter attack late in 1918 that led to an Armistice, or cessation of hostilities, with Germany. Of more long-term concern to the Western powers was the creation of a communist state in Russia. Communist beliefs challenged the ideas of the Western democracies,

who broadly favoured capitalism, the right of individuals to create and keep their wealth, democracy, individual rights and international free trade.

To begin with, the allies tried to intervene in Russia against the Bolsheviks. British, American, French, Canadian and Japanese soldiers intervened in support of the 'White' Russian, anti-Bolshevik forces who were fighting the Bolsheviks and their supporters, known as the 'Reds'. However, the intervention was half-hearted, the majority of Russians favoured the Reds and foreign intervention proved a useful propaganda weapon for the Reds against the Whites. Eventually, the allied forces withdrew, but the Bolshevik leadership did not forget their actions. To the Bolshevik, and eventually the Soviet, leadership this showed that the Western democracies were enemies and were not to be trusted. On the allied side, suspicion of the new communist state and what it stood for meant that America did not even recognise the new government of Russia until 1933. For many historians these events form the basis of the Cold War.

Ideological differences	
capitalism	**communism**
Economic freedom: <ul><li>Encouraged private enterprise</li><li>Companies could be owned by individuals or by shareholders</li><li>Minimal government interference</li></ul>	Economic control: <ul><li>The state owned the economy</li><li>The government owned and planned the economy on behalf of the people</li><li>Large-scale government interference</li><li>Sometimes known as a 'command' economy</li></ul>
Political system: <ul><li>Democratic with personal freedoms, such as the right to vote, regular elections, freedom of speech and the press</li></ul>	Political system: <ul><li>Only one political party allowed, the Communist Party</li><li>Secret police to ensure behaviour and to root out anti-government activity</li><li>Censorship and lack of personal freedoms</li></ul>

Russia between the First and Second World Wars

Events running up to 1939 and the outbreak of the Second World War did little to bring the two sides together. Following the death of Lenin in 1924 there was a power struggle within the Communist Party of the Soviet Union. By 1929, Joseph Vissarionovich Dzhugashvili, who took the name Stalin, or 'man of steel', had emerged as the leader of the Soviet Union.

Stalin was determined to make the Soviet Union strong. To do this he used a series of Five Year Plans to industrialise the country. Within ten years Russia had doubled her economic output and had become a modern industrial nation. However, this economic achievement came at great cost to Russia's population. Many Russians died to fulfil Stalin's aim of a powerful industrial Russia.

Source 1.2

Josef Stalin (1879–1953): a Bolshevik member who was Communist Party Secretary from 1922. He emerged as leader by 1929 after playing his rivals off against each other. He led the massive industrialisation of his country but purged his party and army leadership in the 1930s to stop potential opposition. Stalin led his country during the Second World War and oversaw its emergence as a superpower after 1945.

The years between 1919 and 1939 saw other political beliefs rise and fall. In particular, Fascism emerged in many European countries in the aftermath of the First World War. In Germany, a weak democracy had replaced the rule of the Kaiser (the King) who had ruled Germany up to 1918. A world economic depression in 1929 plunged firstly America, then the world into crisis. Germany was badly affected by this economic crisis and its people turned to radical solutions by voting for the Nazi Party. The Nazis, led by Adolf Hitler, promised to restore German pride after the end of the First World War and the humiliating Versailles Peace Treaty.

In 1933 the Nazi Party came to power in Germany. They immediately started to increase the power of Germany by expanding its military forces and challenging the terms of the Treaty of Versailles. Then, in the years before 1939, Nazi Germany became increasingly aggressive, taking over other countries like Austria and the Czech part of Czechoslovakia. Both the Soviet Union and the Western democracies of France and Britain feared that the other would do a deal with Hitler, leaving them to fight Germany alone. Stalin looked at the actions of the Western democracies towards Nazi Germany with suspicion. Britain and France both gave Hitler most of what he demanded in the mid-1930s. This policy of giving in to German demands for territorial change in order to avoid war is called **appeasement**. Stalin saw such appeasement as weakness and feared that the Soviet Union would have to face Hitler alone.

From the point of view of Britain, France and the United States, Stalin was also untrustworthy. Stalin did a secret deal with Germany in 1939 over Poland. This deal was called the German–Soviet Non-Aggression Pact. In reality, it carved Poland up between Germany and the Soviet Union and led to Hitler's invasion of Poland in September 1939, which triggered the Second World War in Europe. Stalin had become an enemy of the West.

The Second World War

Suspicions between the Soviet Union and the West increased during the early stages of the war, but when Germany invaded the Soviet Union in 1941, Britain rushed to offer aid to the Soviet Union and was soon shipping military material to the Soviets. However, as the war progressed Stalin complained that the help he was getting was not enough and that Soviet forces were doing most of the land-based fighting against Germany. He felt that the allies in the West (America had entered the war in 1941, after Japan bombed her naval base at Pearl Harbour) were deliberately not committing large numbers of ground troops to the invasion of occupied Europe. Stalin wanted this to happen to relieve the pressure on his military forces. It was not until 1944 that a 'Second Front' against the Germans was opened with the invasion of France by the Western allies.

The Eastern Front was the name given to the battlegrounds between Russia and Germany and was horrific in its brutality. It was Soviet forces that held the Germans at the Battle of Moscow and turned the tide of the war. Soviet forces also took Berlin in 1945 after fierce fighting. It was on the Eastern Front, in Russia, that Germany lost, and the Soviet Union won, the Second World War. But Soviet forces as well as her population suffered huge casualties, estimated at around thirty million deaths, during the Second World War. Stalin's desire to protect the Soviet Union from further threat can help explain some of his actions after the war. Stalin's suspicion of his allies was so great that, even in the latter stages of the war, he feared the Western allies would do a deal with Germany and together they would all attack the Soviet Union.

Source 1.3

American and Soviet soldiers meet in Germany. Why were such happy scenes not likely to last?

Differences between the allies about the post-war world

Even while the Second World War was raging, the main allied leaders met to discuss what the future would hold. The first meeting of the 'Big Three' (a term used for the leaders of Britain, America and the Soviet Union: Churchill, Roosevelt and Stalin) took place in the capital of Iran, Tehran, in 1943. This meeting was about how to win the war against Germany, Italy and Japan.

Source 1.4

Winston Churchill (1874–1965): British Prime Minister during the Second World War. Churchill was a passionate anti-communist, but famously said that he would, 'work with the devil if it would help defeat Hitler'. Churchill developed a good relationship with Stalin, but was very suspicious of him after the war. He also gave the famous Iron Curtain speech against the Soviet Union in 1946.

Franklin D. Roosevelt (1882–1945). Roosevelt was the American President from 1933 until his death in 1945. Roosevelt felt that he had a good relationship with Stalin.

Churchill, Roosevelt and Stalin were the 'Big Three' who would decide the post-war world. Why do you think that their views about how to treat Germany after the war might have differed?

By 1944 it was clear that Nazi Germany was going to be defeated. A number of issues began to divide the allies. One of the issues was what to do with countries freed from Nazi rule. This was particularly problematic with regard to Poland and Germany. Both sides saw the world in very different ways. The Western allies wanted countries that had been freed from Nazi rule to hold democratic elections and develop free trade. The Soviet Union was far more concerned with the protection of Russia and with the creation of sympathetic pro-Soviet governments in Eastern Europe as a protective screen against any future aggression from the Western powers. This idea was sometimes called 'creating a buffer zone' because of the way buffers on a rail track take the impact of any speeding train. In this way, Poland would take the hit of any attack towards the Soviet Union as well as giving the Soviets time to prepare a defence against the attack.

The issue of Poland

Poland was a big issue for both Britain and Russia. Britain had gone to war over the German invasion of Poland. Britain was also home to the Polish Government in exile and of significant Polish military units, which had managed to escape from mainland Europe. A Poland free from external influence to which Poles in Britain could return was, ideally, what Britain would like to have seen. Stalin, however, saw Poland very differently. Poland had been the route for three invasions of Russia in the twentieth century. Firstly, by Germany in the First World War, then by those helping the Whites in the Civil War and then by Germany, once again, in the Second World War. Perhaps understandably, Stalin wanted a 'friendly' government in Poland.

By 1944 Soviet forces had pushed German forces back through Poland and were moving on the Polish capital of Warsaw. In August, as Soviet forces approached the city, the Polish resistance movement, called the Home Army, rose up against the Germans in Warsaw. They hoped to free the city from Nazi control without Soviet help. The aims of the Polish resistance were to help with the general attack on German forces and to show Polish independence. Polish forces were allied to the Polish Government in Britain, who wanted to show they had the right to rule in Poland. In the event, Soviet forces stopped their advance before the gates of Warsaw. German forces crushed the Poles and the Soviet forces did nothing to help them, despite pleas from Winston Churchill. The only help for the Polish resistance came from Royal Air Force supply drops and one US Army Air Force drop.

The Western allies were suspicious that this was a deliberate policy of Stalin's to remove Polish resistance fighters who were not communists. Stalin claimed his forces had needed time to rest. However, what is not in doubt is that the German victory saw the defeat of the main Polish military force that backed the Polish Government-in-exile in London. The

Soviet-backed Polish Committee of National Liberation assumed control of the country once Soviet forces eventually continued their offensive through Poland and invaded Germany. A communist-led Provisional Government of Poland was imposed on the country on 1 January 1945. Stalin had gained his 'sympathetic' government.

Conferences at Yalta and Potsdam

There were two meetings between the Big Three (Stalin, Roosevelt and Churchill) in 1945. The first was at Yalta in the Russian Crimea and the second was at Potsdam in Germany.

The meeting at Yalta saw Stalin agree to become allies with the United States and enter the war against Japan once Germany was defeated. There was also agreement on the setting up of a United Nations. However, it also saw disagreements about Poland emerge into the open. Churchill wanted to put the pro-Western Polish Government that was in exile in London into power, but Stalin wanted to put in a pro-Soviet Polish Government. Despite the disagreement Stalin eventually got his way, though he did agree to free and fair elections in Poland which were subsequently ignored. The allies also agreed that Germany should be split into four zones after the war, with France, Britain, the United States and the Soviet Union each supervising one zone. Again, there were disagreements. Stalin wanted massive financial damages from Germany (called reparations) to help pay for the destruction of his country. America and Britain opposed reparations, preferring to support a full German recovery in order to help stimulate economic growth and trade.

By the time of the next meeting at Potsdam the war with Germany had ended. There was also a new American President. President Franklin D. Roosevelt's health declined as the Second World War progressed. He was a chain smoker who by 1945 was visibly frail. He died in America on 29 March 1945. Roosevelt was succeeded by his vice-President, Harry Truman. Truman was far less willing to compromise with Stalin, and the American position in negotiations with Stalin toughened up considerably.

The British war leader Winston Churchill had also been replaced, in this case by the Labour leader Clement Attlee. The Conservatives had lost to the Labour Party in the 1945 election, which Labour won by a large majority. Wartime co-operation was slowly giving way to hostility as characters changed, and without a common enemy to unite them. However, the conference did agree to areas of influence (called spheres) for the victorious powers. Italy was to be in the Western sphere, while Romania, Bulgaria and Hungary went to the Soviet sphere. The sort of governments that each country was to have was unclear, but British and American suspicions of Stalin were heightened with his actions over Poland. Non-communist Polish leaders were arrested and a communist-dominated government emerged in Warsaw as we know.

The Nuclear Age arrives

The atom bomb was first successfully tested on 16 July 1945. The new American President, Harry S. Truman was informed about the existence of this new powerful weapon as he assumed power. When the weapon was successfully tested Truman was delighted with the news. He hoped that the bomb could be used to end the war with Japan swiftly and before the Soviet Union became too involved. Stalin already knew all about the bomb as the American development team had been infiltrated by Soviet spies.

Two atomic bombs were dropped on the Japanese cities of Hiroshima and Nagasaki in August 1945. Japan surrendered soon after. The debate about whether America was right to use the atom bomb has gone on for many years. To the supporters of Truman it saved many American and Japanese lives by removing the need for the American military to invade mainland Japan. To opponents the use of the bomb was an immoral act. For Truman the bomb served another purpose as well as swiftly ending the war. He saw it as giving America more military strength, which could be useful if relations with the Soviet Union declined further – which they did. He also hoped that the weapon would show America's technological superiority and moderate Stalin's aggressive behaviour. However, in reality all the existence of the bomb did was increase Stalin's suspicion of the allied powers further. Stalin knew that Truman and the Americans had wanted to keep the weapon's existence secret from him. To Stalin this was yet more evidence that the Western powers could not be trusted. The future arms race that developed as a result of the exploding of the atom bomb was a practical demonstration of the suspicion with which each side saw the other. It was also a symbolic struggle that would show which competing economic system was best.

Source 1.5

This photo shows the mushroom cloud from the nuclear bomb dropped on Nagasaki. Why did such weapons mean that warfare, and the threat of warfare between the superpowers, had changed forever?

In February 1946 Stalin made a speech to the Supreme Soviet (parliaments of the Soviet Union) where he talked about how the very existence of capitalism made future war inevitable. When the American Government asked for details as well as an analysis of Soviet behaviour they received the so called 'long telegram' from the Deputy Chief of Mission in the US Embassy in Moscow, George Kennan. Kennan's analysis of the Soviet Union was very influential. He argued that the Soviet Union was expansionist in its aims and actions. He wanted to stop any sort of co-operation with the Soviet Union and supported firm action against what he saw as Soviet 'aggression'. These beliefs led directly to the US policy of 'Containment', which meant that the USA would take action to stop the spread of communism. Interestingly, the long telegram argued that Soviet actions, such as taking over Eastern Europe with communist governments, were partly explained by traditional Russian insecurity, though later writings from Kennan also argued that communist ideology had a part to play and that Stalin was seeking to defeat capitalism.

Kennan's analysis found sympathy in the American Government. Active opposition to aggressive communism was becoming more popular as anti-communism developed. Many Americans believed that strength was needed to face an aggressive enemy. They looked at the lessons of appeasement in Europe before the Second World War and decided that weakness in the face of aggression simply encouraged further demands.

Industry in the United States also saw communism as a threat to world trade because of its opposition to capitalism. There was also a degree of self-interest from the armed forces and the industries that supplied them. A continuing military threat meant that there would be further spending on weapons and weapons development. By emphasising the threat from the Soviet Union they ensured that the military was well manned with personnel and well funded with equipment.

However, in reality the Americans totally failed to understand the Soviet point of view. America had not been invaded and had not suffered in the way the Soviet Union had. Soviet actions were therefore explained in American eyes as aggressive action rather than as a desire for defensive security.

The Iron Curtain

Source 1.6

Churchill looks under the 'Iron Curtain'. What did Churchill mean when he described an iron curtain coming down across Europe?

Western fears of communist influence in Europe were made clear when Winston Churchill made a speech in Fulton, Missouri in March 1946. He said: 'From Stettin in the Baltic to Trieste in the Adriatic, an iron curtain has descended across the continent.'

Churchill's speech was partly a call for stronger action against Soviet influence in Eastern Europe. When the Red Army had freed Poland, Czechoslovakia, Hungary, Romania and Eastern Germany from Nazi rule, they found themselves in occupation of a significant part of Eastern Europe. At least sixty Red Army divisions stayed in Eastern Europe. They were to play a part in imposing communist regimes on the region. Stalin wanted sympathetic pro-communist governments in these countries and he got them. The technique was basically the same across Eastern Europe. Stalin encouraged local communists to share power with other political parties in coalition governments. These communists were encouraged to take control of important jobs like positions of power within the police, armed forces, civil service and the media, which meant that any elections could be manipulated. Opposition politicians were arrested. Any further elections got the 'right' result and the communists 'won'.

Even when election results went against the communists the results were ignored. In free elections in Eastern Germany in October 1946, the communists got only 20 per cent of the vote. The communist leader Walter Ulbricht simply ignored the result and the Red Army imposed communist rule over East Germany and East Berlin. In Hungary, the communists worked with a coalition of other political parties to begin with, yet by the end of 1947 the Hungarian Communist Party, led by the hard-line Stalin supporter Mátyás Rákosi, was the only political party that existed. All the other political parties had been accused of being anti-Soviet or pro-Fascist and were disbanded. The communist seizure of power in Czechoslovakia took a little longer and needed a coup to remove non-communists from the government in 1948.

The leaders of these states were pro-Stalin communists and did what Stalin ordered them to do. The East European states under Soviet influence were called satellite states. The role of these allies was twofold: firstly they showed the success of communism as an ideology; secondly these allies provided the Soviet Union with a buffer zone in the event of an invasion from the West.

The Truman Doctrine and Marshall Aid

In March 1947, President Truman made a speech on foreign policy. He stated that:

> *At the present moment in world history nearly every nation must choose between alternative ways of life. The choice is too often not a free one.*
>
> *Our way of life is based on the will of the majority, and is distinguished by free institutions, representative government, free elections, guarantees of individual liberty, freedom of speech and religion, and freedom from political oppression.*
>
> *The second way of life is based on the will of the minority, forcibly imposed upon the majority. It relies upon terror and oppression, a controlled press and radio, fixed elections, and the suppression of personal freedoms.*
>
> *I believe that it must be the policy of the United States to support free peoples who are resisting attempted subjugation by armed minorities or by outside pressures.*

President Truman's speech announced active American involvement to stop the spread of communism. This involvement came in a number of forms, the most important of which was financial aid. However, machinery, food and expertise were also exported to countries that needed it. The American economy had doubled in size during the war. America had also lent large sums of money to many countries fighting the war and now had the wealth to help economies that needed rebuilding after the devastation of the Second World War.

Conflict point: Greece

The country of Greece was the first to see active American involvement. Greece had suffered badly from German occupation during the Second World War. Afterwards there was civil war between the monarchists and communists as each sought to gain power. According to the agreements between the Big Three, Greece was supposed to be an area of British influence. However, at the end of the Second World War Britain could simply not afford the cost of dealing with the civil war in Greece. Britain had fought throughout the war and needed money to rebuild her own industry and housing. When Britain announced that she could no longer aid the Greeks the Americans stepped in to help.

The Americans feared that the Soviet Union was helping the communists. In fact, Stalin gave no help to the Greek communists as he had agreed that Greece was part of the area of Western influence. The Greek communists did receive some help, but this was from communist Yugoslavia. Unlike other East European states, Yugoslavia had freed itself from German rule. Communist partisans, led by Josip Broz Tito, had expelled the Germans from their country by 1945. This allowed communist Yugoslavia to develop a more independent line from the other East European states, which had Stalinist leaders imposed on them. However, American aid and military advisers were sent to support the Greek Government and eventually the communists were defeated. This is a good example of the practical containment of communism that Truman had envisioned in his previous speech on the matter.

The Marshall Plan

America also developed a plan to pump significant economic help into the battered European economies. The American European Recovery Programme became known as the Marshall Plan, after the US Secretary of State, George Marshall. Marshall had travelled through Western Europe in 1947 and had been shocked by what he saw. He believed desperate, hungry people might be persuaded to follow communism so financial and physical help, such as machinery, was pumped into the European economies. The basic idea was that if people had jobs and food they were less likely to be persuaded by communist slogans and promises. However, there was also a selfish motive behind such actions. A growing European economy would be a market for American goods.

Marshall Plan resources were available to all European economies, but they had strings attached. Countries were expected to open up their economies to US capitalist interests and to reject communism. Unsurprisingly, the Soviet Union rejected this offer, seeing it as an attempt to influence her through economic pressure. The other East European states did not join either. Instead, in 1949 Stalin set up the Comecon to co-ordinate East European economic development. Comecon stands for the Council for Mutual

Economic Assistance. In theory this organisation was to provide support for the East European economies. In reality it was a way for the Soviet Union to dominate these states economically by encouraging the expansion of heavy industry and the collectivisation of agriculture in the years after the war.

The United States had spent about $13 billion by the time the Marshall Plan ended in 1951. It had the desired effect in that Western economies began to grow and politically the growth of communism was contained. The Greek communists were defeated and in Italy the powerful communist–socialist alliance was defeated by the right-wing Christian Democrats in elections in 1948. The American secret service, the CIA, had provided significant help to the Christian Democrats during this election. The CIA concluded that their intervention had been successful and had stopped a communist victory. This result would encourage the CIA to interfere in the internal affairs of other countries in the future.

The Berlin blockade, 1948–49

The conferences at Yalta and Potsdam agreed to divide up Germany and its capital city Berlin into four zones, to be administered on a temporary basis by the wartime allies. Berlin was in the middle of the Russian sector. As shown previously a pro-Stalin Communist Government was imposed on East Germany. The East was plundered by the Soviet Union for resources. The West was democratic and began to develop economically due to Marshall Aid. Soon, differences in living standards between East and West Germany as well as East and West Berlin began to grow.

Source 1.7

Areas of Germany and Austria occupied by the allies at the end of the Second World War.

Economic differences developed. The Western powers wanted Germany to become one economic unit. They decided to introduce a new currency in their zones in 1947. The new Deutsche Mark would help bring economic stability and aid recovery. Stalin saw things very differently. He wanted to make sure that Germany would never again threaten Russia. By splitting Germany in two this would permanently weaken her.

This disagreement about currency changes led to Soviet action. In June 1948 all road, rail and canal links with West Berlin were cut. West Berlin was approximately one hundred miles inside the Soviet zone in Germany. The US saw this as an attack on the West and responded with a massive airlift of supplies into Berlin. British and American aircraft flew in 1.7 million tonnes of supplies to feed and heat the West Berliners. Berlin survived and by May 1949 Stalin was forced to accept his strategy had failed and lifted the blockade.

The development of military alliances and the arms race

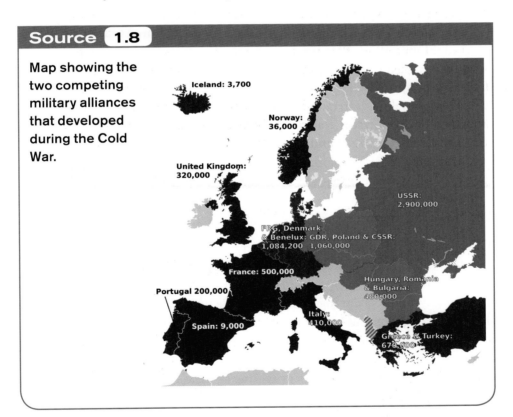

Source 1.8

Map showing the two competing military alliances that developed during the Cold War.

Iceland: 3,700

Norway: 36,000

United Kingdom: 320,000

USSR: 2,900,000

FRG, Denmark & Benelux: 1,084,200

GDR, Poland & CSSR: 1,060,000

France: 500,000

Hungary, Romania & Bulgaria: 480,000

Portugal 200,000

Italy: 410,000

Spain: 9,000

Greece & Turkey: 670,000

One result of the Berlin airlift was the creation of the North Atlantic Treaty Organisation (NATO) in 1949. The Western powers committed themselves to co-ordinated military action in the event of Soviet aggression, therefore NATO was a defensive alliance. For the Western European powers this was a relief, as America was now involved in a peacetime military alliance. The guiding principle of NATO was that an attack on one of its members would

be seen as an attack on all members. This is called 'collective security'. Original members included the USA, Britain, France, Belgium, Holland, Luxembourg, Portugal, Denmark, Iceland, Italy, Norway and Canada.

In 1952, Turkey and Greece joined NATO. However, when West Germany joined in 1955 the Soviet Union created a similar organisation of their own, called the Warsaw Pact, in response. This also stated that Warsaw Pact members would act collectively in defence of socialism if one was attacked. The Soviet Union and her seven satellite states in Eastern Europe now faced NATO in their own military alliance. Europe was now divided into two armed camps. The division between West and East Germany was also formalised with the creation of the Federal Republic of Germany in the West and the German Democratic Republic in the East.

The arms race

As discussed previously, nuclear weapons were used in the Second World War to help defeat Japan, but they also opened up an arms race between the two superpowers as their relationship declined after the war. On 29 August 1949 the Soviet Union successfully exploded its own atomic bomb. They had caught up with the Americans! The Soviets were helped by spies in the West who passed on important information that helped speed up their own nuclear programme. In response the Americans began to develop the hydrogen bomb; its destructive power was considerably greater than the atom bombs dropped on Nagasaki and Hiroshima. A hydrogen bomb was successfully tested in November 1952. The power of the new weapon was extraordinary. When exploded a three-mile wide white fireball shot into the sky. This was accompanied by a wall of heat which could be felt over 15 miles away. Nine months later the Soviets tested their own H-bomb. The era of the thermonuclear bomb had arrived.

The arms race is important for a number of reasons. Firstly, it gave both alliances the military power to totally destroy each other in the event of a nuclear conflict. However, possibly more importantly, the arms race also took on a symbolic meaning. Whichever side was 'ahead' in the race claimed that this was a sign that its economic system, and by implication its ideology, was superior. America saw superior nuclear strength as a way of countering the large Red Army, while America's western allies in Europe saw American nuclear power as providing a shield over them to deter the Soviet Union from attacking. The expansion of America's nuclear arsenal was extraordinary. In 1950, America had 298 atomic weapons. By 1962 this had grown to 27,100. Delivery systems for these weapons also developed.

The Korean War, 1950–53

Although the Cold War was clearly active by 1949, it was a conflict in Korea that showed the increasingly uncompromising positions of both sides. By 1949, another large country had become communist: China. In

1949 Chinese communists, led by Mao Zedong, had defeated the US backed Nationalist forces, called the Kuomintang, and Mao had announced the establishment of the People's Republic of China. To the Americans, the victory of the communists in China seemed to confirm the dangers of worldwide communist expansion. Containment was going to be needed across the world, not just in Europe.

Events during the Korean War showed that both America and the Soviet Union were willing to intervene in foreign conflicts for their own ideological reasons.

Source 1.9

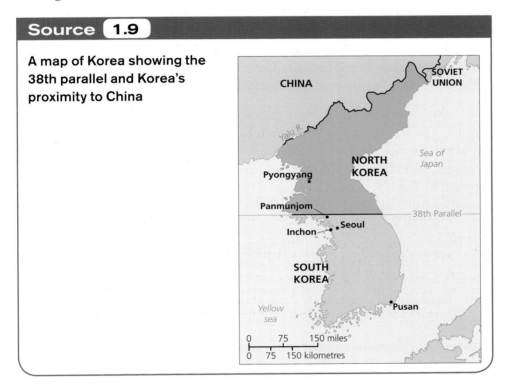

A map of Korea showing the 38th parallel and Korea's proximity to China

Korea

Korea was a Japanese colony from 1910 until the end of the Second World War in 1945. In August 1945 the Soviet Union declared war on Japan and began to attack the northern part of the Korean peninsula. Soviet troops halted on the 38th parallel, a point which had been agreed with the Americans, whose own troops arrived in the southern part of the peninsula in September.

The two parts of Korea developed along ideological lines. The North developed as a pro-communist state, while the South developed along capitalist lines. Both sides claimed to be the rightful government of a united Korea.

Soviet and American military forces withdrew from Korea in 1949. The North launched a full-scale invasion of the South in June 1950. To begin with the war was a civil war, but the Northern forces soon had the weak South Korean forces in retreat. Seoul, the capital of South Korea, fell to

Northern forces in three days. The war now developed in part due to the superpower rivalry of the Cold War.

The Americans interpreted this as a war encouraged by Stalin. There is little evidence for this, but in the context of an American President and people concerned by the spread of communism, action quickly followed. There was anti-communist hysteria in the US and Truman had already been criticised over the loss of China to communism. In response to Northern gains, Truman ordered both air and naval units to South Korea. The United Nations then called on North Korea to withdraw its forces from the South and voted to send help to defend South Korea. The United States used the fact that the Soviet Union was not attending the UN Security Council to get the unanimous agreement needed for action. The Soviet Union could veto any decision made by the Security Council, but was not attending in protest at the UN refusal to allow communist China into the United Nations.

The United States was in effect using the United Nations to justify its own actions. The UN agreed to help South Korea repel the invasion, which paved the way for military intervention from America and fifteen other UN members, including Britain. America made up half of the ground troops supplied by the UN as well as most of the air and naval forces. Troops moved swiftly to Korea, but the North Koreans were tough opponents. By August, South Korean and American forces had been pushed into a small area in the southeast corner of the Korean peninsula around the city of Pusan. The American commander, General MacArthur, landed US marines behind the Northern forces at Inchon. This manoeuvre, plus massive bombing of military targets by American B-29 bombers, turned the tide of war and the Northern forces were pushed back towards the 38th parallel.

However, at this point an interesting decision was made. UN forces pushed into North Korea. The goal now was to unite Korea and in the process, roll back communism. UN forces pushed onto the Yalu River, which formed the border with communist China. China was alarmed at UN actions and felt threatened by the idea of both a unified, capitalist Korea and the likelihood of further active anti-communist actions by America. The Chinese leader Mao Zedong ordered a counterattack. On 27 November 1950 Chinese forces poured over the border into North Korea. The Soviet Union provided air support, which operated in the colours of the People's Republic of China. On land, Chinese forces pushed back the UN forces. However, the UN had air superiority and the massive aerial bombardment of Northern supply lines began to have an effect.

The war eventually ground on into stalemate with neither side able to make the decisive breakthrough. To break the stalemate General MacArthur suggested using atomic bombs against China. This was too much for President Truman, who sacked him and replaced MacArthur with General

Matthew Ridgway. War weariness was also having an effect. A new American President, Dwight Eisenhower, took power in 1953. He wished to bring the war to a close. When Stalin died in March 1953 the new Soviet leadership also pushed for peace.

Peace talks began and a ceasefire was established on 27 July 1953. The front line was now back around the 38th parallel. A 'demilitarised zone' was established around this parallel and is still defended to this day by North Korean troops on one side and South Korean and American troops on the other. An official peace treaty has never been signed.

Why was the Korean War important?

The Korean war was important as it became a part of the greater superpower conflict between East and West. It also saw the emergence of China as a superpower in its own right. Many communists in Asia now looked to it rather that the Soviet Union for leadership. The war also could have escalated into a nuclear conflict if civilian control of the US military had not sacked MacArthur. Furthermore, the 'hot war' of Korea made both sides in the Cold War more determined to protect either communism or capitalism. America, for example, trebled its military spending to deal with what the USA saw as communist aggression across the world, not just in Europe. It is also interesting to note that when the opportunity arose American forces went beyond containment and tried to roll back communism.

Interpretation and argument

As you are no doubt aware, historians disagree about why events happen. The Cold War is no exception to this rule. During this period Soviet historians, unsurprisingly, blamed America and the West for the Cold War. Conversely, in America the Soviet Union was blamed for the Cold War. Historians such as Thomas Bailey argued that Soviet aggression and expansionism after the Second World War had forced the United States into the policy of Containment.

In the 1960s, this view of the Cold War in America was challenged by so-called 'Revisionist' historians. Such views were coloured by the fact that, at this time, America had effectively lost the Vietnam War. This led to some major reassessments of American foreign policy. Revisionists challenged the idea that the Cold War was solely the fault of the Soviet Union. They argued that Soviet actions after 1945 were not expansionist, but were instead the result of wanting to protect themselves from future invasion after the destruction of the Second World War. Other revisionists, such as Walter LaFeber, saw the Cold War in historic terms and argued that its origins lay in trade conflict between America and Russia in the nineteenth century. American actions after the Second World War, aimed at imposing an American economic model on the rest of the world, were blamed as a cause

of many of the conflicts that arose during the Cold War. Historians such as Gar Alperovitz see the conflict starting with the explosion of the atom bombs over Nagasaki and Hiroshima. Alperovitz argues that this was not done to end the war sooner, but rather to impress the Soviet Union and stop her expanding. Two aims in which it clearly failed.

In more recent years, historians have sought to paint a more balanced picture. Historians such as John Gaddis initially pointed out that both sides shared some of the blame for the Cold War. Yet with the opening of the Soviet archives after the collapse of communism, further interpretations have emerged. John Gaddis, for example, has changed his view and now firmly blames the Soviets, and in particular Stalin, for the Cold War.

Activities

1 Using the map and information in this chapter, give an outline account of the main events of the Korean War.

2 Work with a partner. One of you take the side of the North/communists, the other the side of the South/capitalists. What did the Korean War mean for your side? Think about five main consequences then take turns persuading your partner that you are right!

3 Group evidence around the following headings. Write no more than three points per heading but make them specific and detailed.

- Ideological differences
- Tensions within the wartime alliance
- The US' decision to use the atom bomb
- Disagreements over the future of Germany
- The arms race
- Crisis over Korea

Explain why each area caused the Cold War to develop in some way. Make judgements about which area is the most important and which is the least important. In order to make your judgement relevant for an extended response, think about how to back up your statement that a factor is important or unimportant by supporting it with a reason. Why did you make the decisions that you did?

Unit assessment practice

Complete a unit assessment standard:

> European and World Outcome 2 requires you to draw on and apply knowledge and understanding of complex European and World historical issues in a number of ways.

> Assessment standard 2.1 asks you to describe, in detail and with accuracy, the context of a European and World historical issue such as:

Describe the background to the development of the Cold War after the end of the Second World War.

Extended response practice and Top Tip 1

What sort of question will I be asked on this topic?

The answer to that question is easier than you might think. Setters – people who write your exam questions – **must** base their questions exactly on what is written in the SQA descriptor of what this course is about. You already know there can only be four types of essay question asked:

- To what extent … ?
- How important … ?
- A statement followed by 'How valid is this view?'
- How successfully … ?

In topic 1 you are asked to evaluate – or judge – why attitudes changed towards immigration in the 1920s. In other words, you will be asked to judge which of several reasons were the most important. There is no correct answer, so a marker is looking for you to explain all the reasons and then prioritise by deciding if the reason given to you in the question is more or less important than the others. You can make your own mind up which reason or reasons were most important. The important thing to do is make sure you have explained all possible reasons for changing attitudes towards immigration before you make your final decision in response to the question. In this topic it is almost impossible to imagine a question that starts with 'How successfully … ?' These sorts of question are only used when the focus of the unit is on judging the effectiveness of something.

How to get good marks for your extended response

Extended responses on this subject appear in Section 3 of your exam paper. Here is an example of the type of question that you could be expected to answer:

'How important were ideological differences between the USA and USSR in causing the Cold War, up to 1955?'

How well you do depends on the way you respond to the question. Marks are allocated to the various sections of the response.

There are 4 marks for the **structure** of the essay. Structure refers to the introduction and conclusion of the essay. That means how you begin your essay and how you end it. 2 marks are for the introduction and 2 marks are for the conclusion.

Structure: The Introduction

You will get up to 2 marks for your introduction if you do three things:

1   Your introduction must include a **context**. This means that you must set the scene by describing the big picture or background to the issue in the question. In one or two sentence(s) describe the historical topic that the question is based on.

2   You need to give a **line of argument**. The simplest way to do this is to use the words in the question and include the word 'partly'. This instantly shows a marker that you are focusing on the **issue** that the question is asking about but also that you are going to debate the question and examine several factors before you make your decision. So, for the question on page 21 you might say: 'Ideological differences between the USA and USSR were important in causing the Cold War, however, other factors need to be considered.' Notice how the words of the question have simply been reorganised to provide a basic line of argument.

3   You need to make sure that you identify **other areas**, or factors, that you are going to develop in the main part of the essay. This can be done simply as a list. So, to take our example: 'There were other factors that led to the Cold War, such as the arms race, disagreements about the future of Germany and the Korean War.' However, you are better to expand each factor with one sentence on each. To take our example again: 'However, other factors, such as the arms race between the superpowers, led to misunderstandings. Also of importance were disagreements over what should happen to Germany after the war, although this could be said to be a symptom of the broader ideological disagreement.'

Knowledge

6 marks are available for **relevant, detailed knowledge** that is used correctly. You will not get any marks for simply mentioning a fact. The information included has to be relevant to the question, not just to the topic. One way to think about this is to use evidence to support a factor or area that you are developing in the main part of your essay.

One factor you must look at in this essay is the ideological differences between the two superpowers. So, here is a fact: 'The USA believed in capitalism and the USSR believed in communism.' This is a fact, but it is not being used to answer the question, so it needs detail and focus. Here is the fact developed and linked to the factor: 'The USA believed in capitalism and the USSR believed in communism, which caused tension as they were two very different systems of belief.' The fact is linked to the question, gives a little more explanation and is worth one mark. You need to do this sort of thing at least six times to get full marks for knowledge for this question.

Argument: Analysis and evaluation

10 marks are available for the way in which you analyse and evaluate the knowledge in terms of the issue in the question asked. This means that **half** of the marks available for an extended response are for the quality of argument.

There are three different things to do to build up your marks:

1   Analyse your information by commenting on it in a basic way, but relating it more to the topic rather than the exact question – this will gain you up to 4 marks if it is done several times.

2   Develop your analysis by linking your comments about your information directly to the factor you are writing about and how it links to the question. This will allow you to be awarded a further 2 marks, up to 6 marks, rather than only 4 for basic analysis.

3   Evaluate by making a judgement about the main question based on the importance of the factors or show different opinions or interpretations linked to the main question. 1–2 marks can be awarded for isolated evaluative comments AND 3–4 marks can be awarded where the candidate connects the evaluative comments together and links them to the line of argument outlined in the introduction.

Basic analysis (maximum 4 marks)

You will get up to 4 marks if you comment on the information you have included that is relevant to the question.

So, after describing a factor you could add a comment that links this directly to the question by adding: 'This was very effective/important because … ' By using **'because'** you are making sure that you are giving a reason, and by using judgement words like **'very effective/important'** you are giving a relative judgement about it as well.

To continue using the example above: 'The USA believed in capitalism and the USSR believed in communism, which helped cause the Cold War because they were two very different systems of belief which led to misunderstandings and tension.'

Some comment has been made that recognises the question, but it has not addressed the focus of the issue: the 'to what extent' bit of the question. However, a basic analysis has been made. It is worth noticing that knowledge is used to support this analytical point. Successful analysis often uses knowledge.

Why did the Cold War emerge in the years up to 1955?

Make this sort of comment at least four times in your essay to gain up to 4 marks.

Developed analysis can gain up to 6 marks

If your analysis comments are linked to the factor you are explaining in terms of the main question then your analysis can gain up to 6 marks, since it is more than just basic comment on importance to the topic. For example:

'The USA believed in capitalism and the USSR believed in communism, which helped cause the Cold War because they were two very different systems of belief which led to misunderstandings and tension. To a large extent these differences in ideology were the main reason for the outbreak of the Cold War as the disagreements about how to run an economy and political power were behind every other factor.'

Notice the reference directly to the 'its importance' part of the question by the addition of the judgement. Also notice how more factual knowledge is added to support the judgement. Facts and argument go hand in hand.

This is a developed analysis as it relates directly to the question and provides some stronger judgement. You will get 1 mark for each developed analysis and if you do it up to six times in your answer you will get up to a possible total of 6 marks for analysis.

Evaluation (maximum 4 marks)

You will get up to 4 marks for evaluating your information in terms of the question. Evaluation is the judgements you make about the relative importance of the various **factors** in terms of the question, rather than just commenting on the factual details you include about each individual factor.

To take our example once again, you could make an overall judgement that ideology was in fact the most important factor in causing the Cold War and that the other factors could be seen as developments or symptoms of this bigger factor. In other words, you are prioritising your factors by explaining one was more important than the others.

Or you might also evaluate a factor in more depth, pointing out an alternative interpretation. For example: 'Although ideology was important in the disagreements about what should happen to Germany after the war, of more importance to the Soviet Union was the desire to maintain her security after the devastation of the Second World War.'

Yet another way to gain evaluation marks is to compare the opinions of other historians and make a decision, with reasons, why you think one opinion is more important than another.

Structure: The conclusion

The conclusion is worth up to 2 marks.

You will get 1 mark if you just summarise the information you have included in your answer.

You will get 2 marks if you can make judgements that answer the question as well as including a summary.

Here is a suggested structure that should get you 2 marks:

- 'In conclusion, there were many factors that are relevant to the question.
- On one hand … (summarise your information that links to one side of the question).
- On the other hand … (summarise the opposing or different information).
- Overall, the most important … (make a judgement that directly answers the question set. By making the point that one factor is the most important, you are making what is called a **relative judgement**.)'

Now have a go yourself. Here is a different question on this topic:

'The arms race was the main cause of the Cold War. How valid is this view?'

Think about what you would change from the plan outlined above.

Now try to write the essay. This may not be your best essay but lots of essay practice is necessary so that you produce the correct style with the correct structure under pressure in the exam.

If you find it easier at this early stage of the course to write just the introduction then that is fine. In fact, writing a quick introduction to a question is a very effective way of revising and preparing for the exam. It helps you to check that you understand a topic. It is also very useful in improving your structure skills since different titles for extended responses require slightly different introductions.

The Soviet Union and its control of Eastern Europe to 1961

2

In March 1953 Stalin died. This was a shock to many Soviet citizens. Stalin was widely mourned in the Soviet Union and many believed that his time in power had brought the Soviet Union to greatness. There were a number of contenders to succeed him to power, but by 1954 Nikita Khrushchev had emerged as the new leader of the Soviet Union. Khrushchev's victory in becoming leader of the Soviet Union brought a new era to the Cold War.

Nikita Khrushchev

Source 2.1

Nikita Khrushchev (1894–1971) was the leader of the Soviet Union from 1954 until his dismissal in 1964. Khrushchev is seen as the man who changed the nature of the Cold War by promoting the idea of 'socialism with a human face'. He was shrewd and ruthless when needed but could also be unpredictable which caused problems and led to his eventual dismissal.

Khrushchev was a very different character from Stalin. He came from peasant stock and his approach to international relations appeared to see a thaw in the Cold War. He loved to travel and visited Britain in 1956 and America in 1959. In 1955, a summit conference took place in Geneva, Switzerland between many of the world's leading powers. Attending were the United States, Britain, China, France and the Soviet Union. Hopes ran high that greater understanding could be reached as the countries sat down and talked to each other. Such a meeting would not have happened in Stalin's time because of his suspicion of the Western powers and belief that war with the Western powers was inevitable. Khrushchev, on the other hand, developed a policy of 'peaceful coexistence' with the Western powers.

Military confrontation was no longer the way in which the Soviet Union would triumph. Instead, they would concentrate on economic development and show the world the superiority of the communist system. However, there was another side to Khrushchev. He was boastful and a bit of a bully, who was more than capable of threatening nuclear war. In 1956 (as Soviet troops were crushing an uprising in Hungary) British, French and Israeli troops seized the Suez Canal from the Egyptian forces of Gamal Abdel Nasser. These troops soon withdrew as a furious America, which had not been informed of the invasion, privately threatened economic sanctions against Britain and her allies. At the same time Khrushchev publicly threatened Britain and France with 'rocket weapons'. As the troops withdrew, Khrushchev felt it was because of his threats.

Khrushchev's belief that threats could work was to have greater consequences when events in Cuba began to unfold in the early 1960s. However, to begin with Khrushchev seemed to offer some hope of greater understanding between the superpowers. This made a lot of sense to Khrushchev as he had publicly over exaggerated Soviet nuclear capabilities and was very keen to be taken seriously on the international stage. When he was eventually invited to visit America by President Eisenhower, he felt that it was a recognition of the importance and status of the Soviet Union as a world power.

Source 2.2

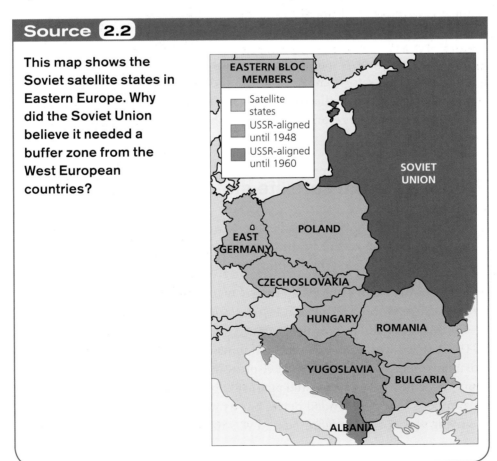

This map shows the Soviet satellite states in Eastern Europe. Why did the Soviet Union believe it needed a buffer zone from the West European countries?

EASTERN BLOC MEMBERS
- Satellite states
- USSR-aligned until 1948
- USSR-aligned until 1960

SOVIET UNION

POLAND

EAST GERMANY

CZECHOSLOVAKIA

HUNGARY

ROMANIA

YUGOSLAVIA

BULGARIA

ALBANIA

Stalin had been ruthless as a leader. He was paranoid and used purges and persecution of his imagined enemies to maintain power. He also encouraged a cult of personality to grow around his leadership and created an idealised view of himself as an all-powerful, all-knowing leader through the use of propaganda and the Soviet media. Once Khrushchev was sure of his power, he sought to challenge Stalin's legacy and to 'de-Stalinise' communism.

In February 1956, Khrushchev shocked the Soviet Union to the core. In a speech to the Twentieth Party Congress held in Moscow, he publicly attacked Stalin's rule, denouncing his crimes and terror. Coming only three years after Stalin's death, the speech caused a sensation across the Eastern Bloc. In the case of the Stalinist leader of the Polish Communist Party, Bolesław Bierut, it had a very immediate effect as he had a heart attack after reading the speech and died.

Khrushchev also had different ideas about how to control the USSR's satellite states. Khrushchev was still a communist, but he suggested that the Soviet model was not the only path the satellites could take. Such suggestions were a real shock to these states. Most of the leaders of the satellite states were concerned by this change. They had been approved by Stalin and used his methods – secret police and camps – to remain in power. Living standards were poor for the majority of the populations in the satellite states and food shortages were common.

Khrushchev's offer of greater flexibility and to show that communism had a human face was soon tested as the populations of the satellite states began to demand actual reform of the political and economic system. How the Soviets reacted to the challenges that arose in their buffer zone of satellite states showed that the reform which Khrushchev encouraged had very specific limits.

Problems in the satellite states

The message from the Soviet leadership worried the leaders of the satellite states. They were hard-line Stalinists who had followed Stalin's orders closely. Events in East Germany illustrated the problem.

The communist leader in East Germany was Walter Ulbricht. He was a strict Stalinist who had forced industrialisation on the East German economy. Heavy industry was developed at the expense of consumer goods. In 1952, when workers were expected to produce more in return for no extra pay there were massive worker protests across East Germany. More than 400,000 workers protested against Ulbricht and his unpopular government. They demanded better pay as well as free elections. However, the rising was not well organised and was easily crushed. Soviet tank units faced the workers and killed and wounded over 400 of them. With the mass arrest of strike leaders the protests stopped. Ulbricht was shaken by these events and introduced some reforms to meet the demands of the strikers. These events can be seen as an early example of demands for change that were to shake the Soviet Union, but would also see a variety of responses.

Events in Poland

Source 2.3

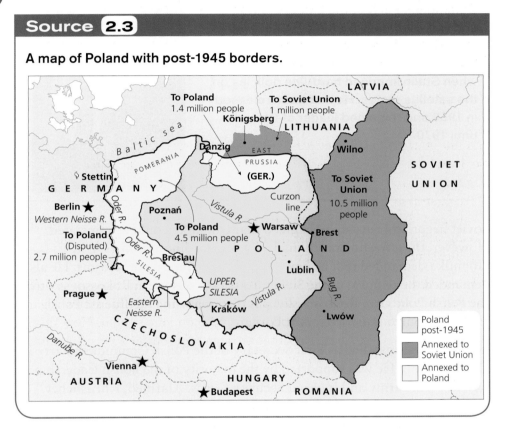

A map of Poland with post-1945 borders.

In Poland the death of their Stalinist leader, Bierut, encouraged reformers to take action. Political prisoners began to be released and pro-Stalin officials were removed from their positions. However, riots soon broke out. Poznan was one of Poland's main industrial cities. In 1956, workers went on strike in protest at wage cuts and poor working and living conditions. These employment protests soon became protests against the Polish Government. The communist government initially reacted with force. Polish tanks and soldiers put down the protests, killing 74 and injuring 300 Polish workers as they did so. However, despite government force the hard-liners did not regain power and reformers brought back a man called Władysław Gomułka and installed him as their leader without Soviet approval.

The Soviet leadership were worried by these events. To begin with the strikers were denounced by the Soviet leadership, who claimed that the

The Soviet Union and its control of Eastern Europe to 1961

protesters had been encouraged by Western agents. However, events were more complex than this. The protests had erupted over genuine grievances – something which many in the Polish Communist Party recognised.

Source 2.4

Władysław Gomułka (1905–1982). Gomułka had been leader of the Communist Party at the end of the war and was genuinely popular. He believed in the idea of different roads to socialism. This had led to his imprisonment in 1951 when Stalin imposed hard-line policies on the satellite states. He had been released in 1956 and remained leader of Poland until 1970.

Soviet negotiators eventually agreed that Gomułka could be reinstated. However, the government still had a lot of hard-line Stalinists in it. Gomułka demanded that he have the power to implement reforms. He also demanded the removal of the Soviet Marshal Konstantin Rokossovsky from the Polish Politburo. Rokossovsky was the man who had ordered Polish troops to confront the strikers at Poznań.

Gomułka was installed as First Secretary of the Polish Communist Party in October 1956. He was supported by the majority of the Polish leadership as well as by the army and Internal Security Corps. Alarmed, Khrushchev decided to intervene directly and made a surprise visit to Warsaw. At the same time, Soviet troops stationed in Poland mobilised and prepared for intervention if the Poles went too far in their demands.

There was a tense meeting between Khrushchev and Gomułka. A worried Khrushchev threatened to use force to maintain Soviet control; Gomułka replied that the Polish Army and people would resist if this happened. However, he also stressed to Khrushchev that the Polish demands were a direct result of Khrushchev's own support of the 'many roads to socialism' idea. He was merely doing what Khrushchev had seemed to encourage.

Khrushchev had enough sense to recognise the opposition he faced and importantly, Gomułka promised that Poland would remain communist and a loyal member of the Warsaw Pact. The Soviets were reassured by this as the buffer zone would remain intact. Soviet troops returned to their barracks. The situation calmed down and Gomułka fulfilled his promise;

Poland remained a faithful ally of the Soviet Union, for the time being at least. In return, Poland was allowed a degree of freedom in order to make its own economic decisions. For example, Polish agriculture did not collectivise in the way other communist countries' agriculture did. Trade was even encouraged with the capitalist West! Some political prisoners were freed and there was a relaxation of censorship. It is, however, important to recognise that Poland remained a communist dictatorship. National feeling in Poland had been controlled, but it had not gone away and would re-emerge in the 1980s.

It is no surprise that there were risings across Eastern Europe as a result of promises for greater freedom. In one sense Khrushchev can be blamed for this as he did offer a form of hope to people who were living in very controlled regimes. However, as events in Poland showed, there were limits to what was allowed. Although the Soviet reaction to events in Poland threatened to become violent they had enough sense to listen to Polish demands and react appropriately. In many ways this was a success, as Poland remained communist and a member of the Warsaw Pact. As future events were to show, this remained the main measure as to how the Soviets would react.

Events in Hungary, 1956

Hungary had been allied to Nazi Germany during the Second World War. After 1945, Hungary had a brief period when she was a multi-party democracy. However, in common with other East European states occupied by Soviet forces, she eventually became a communist state, under the control of Mátyás Rákosi.

Rákosi was a hard-line Stalinist and Hungary's economy developed along Stalinist lines. After the war Hungarian agricultural and industrial goods were sent to the Soviet Union, rather than made available to the Hungarian people. Her cultural traditions were ignored as were her historic traditions and long-standing connections with the West. The repressive police state imposed by Rákosi on the people of Hungary was among the most severe in Eastern Europe. Khrushchev had arranged for the removal of Rákosi from power in July 1956. However, this was not enough for the Hungarians who, inspired by events in Poland, began to demand much more.

The Hungarian students, in particular, had been politicised by recent events. From 1955, independent Hungarian writers and literary organisations developed, the most famous of which was the Petöfi Circle. They were encouraged by Khrushchev's speech and by the 'resignation' of Rákosi in July 1956. In October 1956, Hungarian students from the Technical University protested in Budapest in support of the Poles. Many of the protesters had cut the communist coat of arms out of their Hungarian

national flags. By 6 p.m., the crowd of protesters numbered more than 200,000 and the protest had turned into a protest against the communist government. The protesters were met with bullets from the hated Hungarian Secret Police, known as the ÁVH. The communist government condemned the demands but many of the Hungarian troops sent in to support the ÁVH went over to the crowd. Events looked to be running out of control. The statue of Stalin in the centre of Budapest was pulled down. Ernő Gerő, the Hungarian Prime Minister, called for Soviet help to restore order.

On 25 October 1956, Soviet troops entered Budapest and fierce fighting erupted. The existing Hungarian Government collapsed. A new government had to be formed that held the confidence of the Hungarian people. The person who looked most likely to fulfil this role was Imre Nagy. Nagy had been Prime Minister until 1955. He was brought back into government as Prime Minister, as was János Kádár as First Secretary of the Communist Party. Both Nagy and Kádár had previously been purged from the Communist Party. It was hoped that their involvement in the government would end the protesters' demands for political change. Such a move had helped control events in Poland when Gomułka returned to power, but Hungary was different.

Nagy attempted to control the situation. He called for an immediate end to fighting and promised political and economic reform. He also promised Khrushchev that Hungary would remain loyal to Moscow. The Soviet leadership was split on what to do next. Some wanted to control the reform movement while others wanted to crush the uprising. In the short term, Khrushchev ordered the withdrawal of Soviet troops from Budapest on 28 October. However, more Soviet troops were massed along the border with Hungary just in case, watching how events would unfold.

In fact, the new Hungarian Government could not control events across Hungary. There was too much anger. Strike action spread across the country as industrial workers seized public buildings and formed revolutionary councils. Attacks were made on Soviet troops and many members of the Hungarian Army defected to the protesters, taking their weapons with them.

Carried along by events, Nagy's Government reacted. Nagy announced an end to the one party state. He would form a coalition government and promised free elections. However, on 1 November he went too far. Up until this point the Soviet response had been quiet. Their news agencies spoke of Hungarian workers having 'justified' complaints. But on 1 November Nagy demanded the withdrawal of Soviet troops from Hungary and the withdrawal of Hungary from the Warsaw Pact. He then proposed Hungarian neutrality in the Cold War and contacted the United Nations. This went too far for the Soviets.

Source 2.9

A dead 'escapee' on the Berlin Wall.

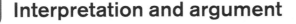

Interpretation and argument

Soviet control of Eastern Europe was interpreted by most Western historians as evidence of their desire to spread communism. The methods used to expand and maintain this control, even in the face of widespread protest, were further evidence of aggressive Soviet intent. Such views were challenged in the 1970s by revisionists writing in the aftermath of the Vietnam War. These writers, such as William A. Williams, emphasised the Soviet need for security in explaining their actions in Eastern Europe, especially in the face of a more economically prosperous West. Unsurprisingly, Soviet interpretations emphasise the view that Soviet actions were driven by a need to protect the Revolution from capitalist aggression. It is no surprise that this line was used to justify both the intervention in Hungary and the building of the Berlin Wall, claiming that the West was behind the Hungarian rising and Western actions provided the need to build a wall around West Berlin to isolate it. In contrast, those in the West saw Soviet actions as evidence of the failure of communism. Popular protests in Poland, Hungary and Berlin had shown the reality of life for many in the communist East as well as the methods that were needed to control the satellite states. The fact that military intervention and a wall were needed showed the economic and political failure of communism.

The Cold War 1945–1989

Activities

You have to make an assessment as to the success of Soviet policies towards their East European satellites in the years before 1961.

In your notes create a grid like the following. Make sure you complete all sections and think about short and long-term arguments to support each viewpoint.

Event	What did the Soviets do?	Arguments that Soviet actions were successful	Arguments that Soviet actions were unsuccessful
1956 Polish rioting			
1956 Hungarian rising			
1961 Berlin crisis			

Unit assessment practice

Complete a unit assessment standard:

European and World Outcome 1 asks you to evaluate the impact of historical developments in a number of ways.

Assessment Standard 1.1 asks you to interpret complex historical information.

Source A

Source A is from a list of demands compiled by students at Budapest Technological University, 23 October 1956.

'We demand immediate evacuation of all Soviet troops.'

'We demand the election by secret ballot of all Party members from top to bottom, and new officials at all levels of the Hungarian Workers' Party (Communist Party).'

'A new Government must be established under the direction of Comrade Imre Nagy. All the criminal leaders of the Stalin–Rákosi era must be immediately relieved of their duties.'

'We demand that general elections, by universal secret ballot, be held throughout the country to elect a new National Assembly, with all parties participating. We demand that the right of the workers to strike be recognised.'

1   Use at least four pieces of information from Source A and at least two
    points from your own knowledge to explain why there was demand for
    reform in Hungary by 1956.

Extended response practice and Top Tip 2

Writing a successful introduction

At the end of Chapter 1 you may have seen a top tip providing general
advice on how to write a good extended response. At the end of this chapter
and all the others in this book you will find more top tips giving more
detailed advice about certain parts of your extended response. This top tip
is about writing a good introduction.

The examples provided here all relate to the topic of this section which is:
An assessment of the effectiveness of Soviet policy in controlling Eastern
Europe up to 1961.

When you are preparing for the exam think very carefully about the style of
question you will be asked and what the question will be about. In this top
tip **all** the extended response example questions will be about the issue
mentioned above. In simple English the issue means – how effectively did
the USSR keep control over Eastern Europe in the years up to and including
1961?

To be sure about what the questions you might be asked on the Cold War
topic, check with the SQA website. The detail for Section 2 of the Cold War
topic is: 'The desire for reform in Eastern Europe; differing Soviet reactions
to events in Poland (1956), Hungary (1956) and Berlin (1961); domestic
pressures; the international context; military and ideological factors.'

You should also know about the style of question you will be asked. There
are only three styles of question you can be asked for this topic.

1   One style is to start with, 'To what extent … ', such as, 'To what extent
    did the Soviet Union effectively control Eastern Europe, up to 1961?'

2   Another style is to provide a statement about the effectiveness of Soviet
    policy in controlling Eastern Europe up to 1961, followed by the
    question, 'How valid is this view?' An example would be: 'Soviet
    reaction to the desire for reform in Eastern Europe in the years up to
    1961 was effective. How valid is this view?'

3   Finally, there is a third style of question that asks, 'How successfully … '
    An example could be: 'How successfully did the Soviet Union deal with
    challenges to its power in Eastern Europe up to 1961?'

Now start planning an introduction to this question:

'How successful was the Soviet response to events in Eastern Europe up to
1961?'

First of all think about the **topic**. What do you have to know about to answer this question? You might think the answer is obvious ... and it is! But under exam pressure people can become confused and lose marks and time by writing about irrelevant subjects. So the topic of this question is how the Soviet Union reacted to challenges to its power in Eastern Europe up to 1961.

The next thing to think about is the **task**. In other words, what you have to do to answer the question successfully. The **context** will not change as it is background to the topic. The **factors** will not change for this extended response, *but* the **line of argument** will change depending on the question asked.

How you answer this question is almost exactly the same as you answer any other question on this topic.

Remember your introduction must have a context: a line of argument that is focused on the demands of the question and outlines the factors you will develop in your essay.

Your context should last about two sentences and briefly outline the background to the question. In this case, you should outline why challenges to Soviet power emerged in the 1950s and early 1960s. You must include relevant information, so a brief description of relations between the USSR and Eastern Europe in the 1950s could start like this:

'The death of Stalin in 1953 led to the emergence of Nikita Khrushchev as Soviet leader. His policies of de-Stalinisation and different paths to socialism encouraged the East European states to seek greater freedom.'

That's all you need for a context – one or two sentence(s).

You should now include a line of argument which opens out your answer and prepares for a full answer to the question – not just a description of events. Your line of argument could indicate that while the challenges to Soviet control were serious there were others that were not so serious. That is a simple line of argument but it means that you cannot lose a mark for not having a line of argument. Here is an example of how your introduction can combine your context with a line of argument.

(**Context**) The death of Stalin in 1953 led to the emergence of Nikita Khrushchev as Soviet leader. His policies of de-Stalinisation and different paths to socialism encouraged the East European states to seek greater freedom.

(**Line of argument**) The Soviet Union's reaction to events in Eastern Europe was successful to a large extent.

You must also include factors to develop, which means that you must outline the main parts of your answer that you will develop in the rest of

your essay. These main 'headings' are easy to include because they are exactly the same things mentioned in the illustrative examples for this section of the Cold War Topic. They are:

- the desire for reform in Eastern Europe
- differing Soviet reactions to events in Poland (1956), Hungary (1956) and Berlin (1961)
- domestic pressures
- the international context
- military and ideological factors.

What now follows is an entire introduction with the three essential parts – context, line of argument and factors to develop all together. Each factor is numbered for you to show how they can fit together as part of an introduction and also as an outline guide for you to follow as you write your essay.

(**Context**) 'The death of Stalin in 1953 led to the emergence of Nikita Khrushchev as Soviet leader. His policies of de-Stalinisation and different paths to socialism encouraged the East European states to seek greater freedom.

(**Line of argument**) The Soviet Union's reaction to events in Eastern Europe was successful to a large extent.

(**Factors to develop**) For example, in 1956 changes within Poland at first alarmed the USSR when the Poles announced their own road to socialism, but in reality there was little challenge to Soviet authority and their reaction was effective. On the other hand, events in Hungary in 1956 were a direct challenge to Soviet control as was increased tension in Berlin, which could not be allowed to continue. Soviet reaction to these crises was successful as they controlled the situations, but there was a cost.'

Another possible question on Section 2 of the Cold War topic is:

'Soviet policies in Eastern Europe were very successful in the period up to 1961. How valid is this view?'

The Cuban Missile Crisis of 1962

3

As the young American President Kennedy met the Soviet leader Khrushchev in Vienna in 1960, he did so in the knowledge that American-backed Cuban exiles had failed to topple a reformist Cuban Government under Fidel Castro. As the Berlin Crisis was developing, so Cuba also began to concentrate the minds of the superpowers. The crisis that developed between 16 and 28 October 1962 is arguably the closest that the world has come to nuclear war.

Cuba

Source 3.1

Cuba is an island situated in the Caribbean, only 90 miles away from the American mainland. The history of Cuba had been one of domination by foreign powers. It had been part of the Spanish colonial empire, but in 1898 the Americans defeated the Spanish after a ten week war. The island then

came under the influence of America. In the following years American businesses invested heavily in the country and dominated many industries, in particular those associated with the production of sugar. In 1959 the country was ruled by General Fulgencio Batista. He had seized power in an armed coup in 1952. Batista's rule of the country favoured the wealthy landowners who dominated sugar production and many American companies were awarded contracts in Cuba by his government. These were often very lucrative. Indeed, American companies owned many sugar plantations as well as having interests in both the mining and cattle farming industries. Relations with the American Government were close and they helped Batista with financial and military aid. By the 1950s the corrupt and dictatorial Batista was extremely unpopular among the ordinary Cuban citizens who endured grinding poverty while Batista and his allies lived in relative wealth. Batista reacted to any sort of opposition harshly. There was censorship of the media and widespread use of torture, for example.

Fidel Castro and Cuba

Opposition to the Batista regime was led by Fidel Castro, a young lawyer who had made an unsuccessful bid to seize power in 1953. He was arrested and imprisoned and then forced into exile in Mexico. However, he returned to Cuba in 1956 and waged a guerrilla war (a guerrilla war is one where small groups of fighters use military tactics such as hit-and-run and ambushes against a larger military enemy) against Batista's forces. Castro was personally charming and he had important allies, in particular a young Argentinian revolutionary called Ernesto 'Che' Guevara. Castro's forces slowly grew in size and popularity, until Batista, recognising the challenge he faced, fled the country on 1 January 1959. A week later Castro's forces entered the Cuban capital, Havana.

Source 3.2

Fidel Castro (1926–2008). Castro led the revolt against Batista which led to his overthrow in 1959. As Castro's relationship with America then deteriorated he turned to the Soviet Union for practical help. The Cuban revolution developed along communist lines.

At this stage Castro was not a revolutionary socialist. The first government he formed was a coalition of groups that supported Cuban nationalism, without necessarily being socialist. However, events were soon to change this. Castro introduced reforms that were unpopular with the Americans. He aimed to redistribute wealth more fairly and improve standards of health and education for ordinary Cubans. In doing this he began to challenge the interests that American businesses had built up in Cuba. In 1960, Castro signed a trade agreement between Cuba and the Soviet Union. Castro then planned to put many American investments in Cuba under Cuban government control (a process known as nationalisation). This involved the seizure of large sugar plantations owned by American businesses. This was unacceptable to American businesses and caused a reaction in America. President Eisenhower announced an economic blockade of Cuba and refused to buy the all-important sugar crop. The Soviet Union saw an opportunity and stepped in to buy the sugar. When America refused to sell fuel to Cuba the Soviet Union stepped in once again to help and provide fuel. Events effectively forced Castro into the embrace of communism. When the two men met at the United Nations in 1960 Castro was embraced by Khrushchev as a fellow revolutionary. This worried America.

American foreign policy and Cuba

The Americans were used to seeing Central and Latin America as their area of influence. They were also willing to intervene in order to make sure that governments in the area were pro-American. For example, in 1954 the American intelligence service, the CIA, had helped to remove a government in Guatemala that the USA did not approve of. By 1961, Castro's Government was also the subject of American intelligence plots to remove Castro and replace his government with one that was sympathetic to the USA. President Eisenhower had approved CIA plans to train a force of anti-Castro Cuban exiles who were to lead resistance to Castro's Government. These plans were inherited by John F. Kennedy when he became American President in 1961. Kennedy was not against the plan, but he was very specific about the amount of help he was willing to offer. In particular, Kennedy did not want to provide any direct American military assistance. American help for the anti-Castro Cubans was to be secret. As a result, US military training for these anti-Castro Cuban forces took place in the jungles of Guatemala. The CIA was confident that when they landed on mainland Cuba the population would rise up against Castro and his supporters. Meanwhile, direct American military help was limited to some disguised American bombers (they were painted in Cuban Air Force colours) which were supposed to destroy the Cuban Air Force.

The Bay of Pigs

When 1500 CIA trained Cuban exiles landed at the Bay of Pigs on the west coast of Cuba in April 1961, American hopes of a successful uprising against Castro swiftly ended.

The Cuban people did not support the invading Cuban exiles. There was no uprising against Castro and the American-trained Cuban forces did not even get off the beach they landed on. Cuban armed forces, equipped with Soviet tanks, battered them and after three days of fighting the exiles surrendered. The whole scheme had been a disastrous failure and it was clear that the Americans, and in particular the CIA, had miscalculated badly. They had totally misjudged the mood of the Cuban people and the abilities of the Cuban military forces. The crisis had a number of consequences.

The crisis united the Cuban people behind Castro, especially when it became clear that the invasion had been part of an American plot to overthrow him. Castro made it clear that his government was now pro-communist and, since he was worried about the possibility of further American attacks, Castro looked for, and received, support from his most important ally, the Soviet Union. America had effectively pushed Cuba towards the Soviet Union through its actions.

The USA on the other hand now saw Cuba as a major threat that had to be dealt with in some way. It was an example of the spread of communism that must be opposed; plus the island was only 90 miles from the mainland of the United States. Kennedy was also determined not to be seen as 'weak' by his political opponents in the USA. As a result, America continued to develop schemes to change the Cuban Government under the codename 'Operation Mongoose'. For example, in 1962 the American military began planning an invasion of Cuba as well as practising amphibious landings. Castro was no fool and understood the message he was being sent by the Americans.

Although the Soviets were delighted by the unexpected opportunity that having a communist Cuba gave them, especially when it was so close to the American mainland, they were also concerned. Khrushchev had met Kennedy in Vienna in June, just a few weeks after the Bay of Pigs shambles. Khrushchev drew some incorrect conclusions regarding Kennedy from the Bay of Pigs. He believed Kennedy was an indecisive and weak leader who was badly advised. The Soviets thought that after the lack of American intervention over the building of the Berlin Wall and the recent Bay of Pigs fiasco they could push for more advantages over America. In particular, if the Soviet Union could place nuclear missiles in Cuba, Khrushchev hoped that the threat of these weapons might divert American attention from Berlin, split NATO and provoke the United States into taking some military

action that would justify a Soviet seizure of West Berlin. It may also have provided a bargaining counter to persuade the Western powers to withdraw from Berlin itself. Khrushchev was also aware that Soviet military forces were inferior to the American ones in terms of nuclear weaponry. Cuba offered an opportunity to reduce the American advantage in this area. Such considerations meant that Cuba had to be protected.

Khrushchev was also concerned to protect Cuba from the threat of future American invasion. It was hoped that a communist Cuba would inspire other Latin American countries to change their governments and become communists. In his memoirs Khrushchev stated that:

> *We were sure that the Americans would never reconcile themselves to the existence of Castro's Cuba. They feared, as much as we hoped, that a Socialist Cuba might become a magnet that would attract other Latin American countries to Socialism. Given the continual threat of American interference in the Caribbean, what should our own policy be?*

> *This question was constantly on my mind. We had an obligation to do everything in our power to protect Cuba's existence as a Socialist country and as a working example to the other countries of Latin America. It was clear to me that we might very well lose Cuba if we didn't take some decisive steps in her defence.*

In July 1962, Castro visited Moscow to negotiate defence agreements with the Soviet Union. Russian advisers, technicians and engineers were sent to help the Cubans. A Russian military base was also established in Cuba. The Americans could do little to oppose this as the relationship was purely defensive at this time. However, Khrushchev's mind was continuing to work. Cuba and its close proximity to the American mainland was an excellent opportunity for him to do something to help the Soviet Union militarily and become the superior superpower.

The arms race and Cuba

During the 1950s, Khrushchev had made a series of claims regarding the superiority of the Soviets in terms of strategic nuclear weapon production. He claimed that the Soviet Union was producing strategic nuclear weapons 'like sausages'. The reality was somewhat different. The Americans had built up a clear superiority in the production of ICBMs (Intercontinental Ballistic Missiles) over the Soviets, and her NATO allies provided bases for American weapons that directly threatened the Soviet Union.

Khrushchev states in his memoirs that:

> We had to think up some way of confronting America with more than words. We had to establish a tangible and effective deterrent to American interference in the Caribbean. But what exactly? The logical answer was missiles. The United States had already surrounded the Soviet Union with its own bomber bases and missiles. We knew that American missiles were aimed against us in Turkey and Italy, to say nothing of West Germany. Our vital industrial centres were directly threatened by planes armed with atomic bombs and nuclear missiles tipped with nuclear warheads. I found myself in the difficult position of having to decide on a course of action which would answer the American threat, but which would also avoid war. Any fool can start a war, and once he's done so, even the wisest of men are helpless to stop it – especially if it's a nuclear one.

The Soviet Union, however, did have a lot of Medium Range Ballistic Missiles (MRBMs). By placing these on Cuba, without the knowledge of the Americans, it was hoped that a credible threat would be created and the Soviet Union would at least have parity with the United States. Such missiles would be able to hit the vast majority of American cities. Khrushchev hoped that when the Americans realised the missiles were in place they would, and could, not react for fear of a direct nuclear attack. Khrushchev continued:

> The installation of our missiles in Cuba would, I thought, restrain the United States from precipitous military action against Castro's government. In addition to protecting Cuba, our missiles would have equalised what the West likes to call, 'the balance of power.' The Americans had surrounded our country with military bases and threatened us with nuclear weapons, and now they would learn just what it feels like to have enemy missiles pointing at you; we'd be doing nothing more than giving them a little of their own medicine. And it was high time America learned what it feels like to have her own land and her own people threatened.

Cuba as a distraction from Khrushchev's domestic problems

A foreign policy success would help protect Cuba and help win the arms race, but it also had a role in helping Khrushchev domestically. Khrushchev had problems at home. His domestic programme of reform, especially

agricultural reform, had not been a great success. He was also being criticised by hard-liners for his de-Stalinisation programme. At the same time, communist China was beginning to pursue a more independent line politically and in international relations. The Chinese were very suspicious of the de-Stalinisation campaign and increasingly felt that they were the true defenders of communism. Khrushchev was also increasingly alarmed at the way in which China was gaining influence in Cuba. Castro had got rid of a pro-Soviet group in May 1962, for example. Khrushchev felt that a foreign policy victory, in the form of missiles on Cuba, would help reassert Soviet authority over Cuba, ensure Castro's loyalty to Moscow and help Khrushchev gain much needed popular and political support at home.

Cuba was approached and Fidel Castro agreed to the missile placement. In July 1962, 65 Soviet ships set sail for Cuba. Ten of the ships carried short and medium range nuclear weapons. Missile sites on mainland Cuba began to be constructed. Despite the construction being surrounded by secrecy, the Americans identified the sites through aerial surveillance and their analysis of the photographs identified the potential nuclear threat. For example, the American reconnaissance flights over Cuba by U-2 spy planes in October 1962 identified a missile base under construction near San Cristobal in western Cuba.

Source 3.3

This is a CIA-labelled photograph of the base at San Cristobal. The photograph was taken from a low-level surveillance sweep by US aircraft. Using this image, can you explain the importance of spy plane photographs during the Cuban Missile Crisis?

MEDIUM RANGE BALLISTIC MISSILE BASE IN CUBA
SAN CRISTOBAL
LAUNCH POSITION
MISSILE-READY TENTS
MISSILE ERECTORS
LATE OCTOBER

Khrushchev's miscalculation of President Kennedy

The early months of the Kennedy presidency had been troublesome for the Americans. There was the embarrassment of the failed Bay of Pigs landings against Castro as well as the fact that the Soviet Union had managed to place the first man into orbit around the Earth during 1961. (The Russian cosmonaut Yuri Gagarin successfully orbited the Earth on 12 April 1961 in his Vostok spacecraft.) Such developments had a symbolic importance and were used by the Soviets to show their supposed technological superiority to the Americans.

Kennedy's first meeting with Khrushchev at the Vienna summit of June 1961 was also badly handled by the Americans. One of the main issues of the meeting was the status of Berlin. Khrushchev was keen to push the Americans into withdrawing their troops from Berlin and for all of Berlin to belong to East Germany. In order to push Kennedy, Khrushchev threatened to sign a separate peace treaty recognising East Germany. He also stated that Berlin should be neutral and that American forces should leave within a year. Khrushchev came at Kennedy strongly and even threatened war. An astonished Kennedy reacted, stating that the American presence in Berlin had been agreed at the end of the war and that American security was linked to that of Berlin. This was one of those times when Khrushchev threatened and blustered. He also concluded that Kennedy was a weak and inexperienced leader who he could dominate. Berlin continued to dominate international politics and Khrushchev's impression of Kennedy as weak was further encouraged when there was only a diplomatic response to the unopposed building of the Berlin Wall later in 1961.

In the event, Khrushchev totally misjudged Kennedy and how he would react to the crisis. He should have realised this earlier as Kennedy announced a massive increase in US military spending, albeit mostly on conventional weapons, in July 1961. Kennedy also called Khrushchev's bluff over claims of Soviet missile superiority when he let it be known that America's nuclear capability was at least as large as the Soviets, if not larger. Khrushchev had previously boasted that the Soviets were producing nuclear weapons like sausages. However, United States intelligence and surveillance confirmed that such claims were fantasy and not backed up by the reality on the ground. At this time, America had at least eight times the number of useable nuclear weapons that the Soviet Union had. However, a nuclear weapon is a nuclear weapon and the close proximity of even a limited number of nuclear weapons in Cuba, so near to the American mainland, was going to be unacceptable to the Americans. Kennedy was not going to be bullied by Khrushchev.

In the aftermath of the Bay of Pigs fiasco, the American President was also determined to be seen as tough against communism to counter the criticism of many Republican Senators that he was doing nothing about Cuba. He set up a small group of senior officials to oversee the American response. This was the Executive Committee of the National Security Council, or ExComm for short. The siting of nuclear missiles on Cuba was unacceptable to Kennedy and ExComm for fairly obvious reasons. Primarily, even medium-range Soviet missiles stationed in Cuba could hit most of the large cities in the USA in the event of nuclear war. The second reason was the old fear about communist expansion. Latin America was very close to Cuba and had traditionally been an area of American influence. The presence of a nuclear-protected and communist Cuba exporting revolution into an area that was considered to be 'America's backyard' was a great concern to American policy makers.

American reaction

Kennedy and his advisers at ExComm debated what to do. Doing nothing was not an option to a president who was only a few weeks away from mid-term congressional elections, where his Democratic Party colleagues would have been wiped out if there had been inaction from Kennedy's administration. The removal of nuclear forces from Cuba was the aim of all members, but they disagreed about how this was to be done. In the end there were two main options that ExComm debated.

- Some of Kennedy's military advisers wanted military action, in particular a devastating air strike that would destroy the missile sites and their defences.
- Others in ExComm, including the President's brother Robert (or 'Bobby') Kennedy and the Secretary of Defence, Robert McNamara, suggested a blockade of Soviet ships going to Cuba. This would buy time for both sides and allow for more diplomatic avenues of contact with the Soviet leadership.

On 21 October, the President backed the option to blockade Cuba. It was decided to call this a 'quarantine' around Cuba as it sounded less threatening.

On 22 October, Kennedy spoke to the American nation on television. He revealed the existence of the missiles on Cuba and announced a naval blockade of the island. The world appeared to be on the brink of nuclear war. Behind the scenes feverish diplomatic activity was taking place between the Americans and Russian diplomats in America. In reality, 24 nuclear warheads had already arrived in Cuba before the blockade was put in place. These medium-range SS-4 nuclear missiles were soon operational and ready to fire.

Source 3.4

The picture shows a newspaper headline after Kennedy's address to the nation regarding Soviet attempts to place nuclear missiles on Cuba. How would you summarise the arguments for and against a blockade?

The Soviets reacted angrily to the blockade and Khrushchev contacted Kennedy to state that the American actions were an act of aggression. However, Khrushchev's plan had been uncovered by the Americans. Khrushchev had no plan B, so ordered the Soviet ships to slow, then stop on 24 October. The American military prepared for an invasion of Cuba, moving 25,000 marines and 100,000 other troops into position. Two massive United States aircraft carriers, *Enterprise* and *Independence*, headed for Cuba at full speed.

Diplomatic efforts to create a face-saving compromise for both sides continued. The United Nations demanded that both sides hold back from action that could lead to war. In reality the important negotiations occurred directly between the Soviets and Americans. The role of Bobby Kennedy was particularly important as was that of the Soviet Ambassador to America, Anatoly Dobrynin. The key event in solving the crisis was Khrushchev's belief that the events were getting out of hand. Khrushchev sent two messages with proposed solutions to the Americans. In the first, a long and rambling letter, he proposed that the Soviets would withdraw their missiles if the US agreed not to invade Cuba. This would remove the reason for the Soviets wanting to site missiles in Cuba. The Americans were very interested in this proposal and further negotiations between Bobby Kennedy and Dobrynin brought American missiles placed in Turkey into play. When Dobrynin raised them as an issue, Kennedy agreed that they could be considered in any solution. The next day a second letter arrived making a new proposal. It stated that the Americans must withdraw their missiles from Turkey in return for the Soviet removal of missiles from Cuba. The American military was outraged, however this proposal merely reflected the negotiations that had been taking place.

The Cuban Missile Crisis of 1962

Meanwhile, military tension increased between the two sides. An American U-2 spy plane strayed into Soviet airspace causing Soviet MiG fighter aircraft to be scrambled. A second U-2 spy plane was shot down over Cuba, killing its pilot. The Americans had agreed that if their U-2 was shot down they would attack. Thankfully they took the view that this was an accident and President Kennedy ordered the American military not to retaliate. On 27 October, Kennedy and his advisers decided to ignore the second letter from Khrushchev and reply to the first one, agreeing to Khrushchev's proposal to withdraw Soviet missiles in return for American assurances they would not invade Cuba. Privately it was also agreed that America would remove its Jupiter nuclear missiles from Italy and Turkey. In 1963 these missiles were quietly removed, though in reality the missiles were obsolete anyway and had served no useful military purpose. Khrushchev accepted the American proposals and American U-2 reconnaissance showed that the Soviets were dismantling their missiles and support equipment on Cuba. The crisis was over.

The results of the Cuban Missile Crisis

In America the settlement was seen as a major foreign policy success for President Kennedy and a defeat for the Soviet Union. Kennedy could claim that he had seen off aggressive Soviet action and forced the removal of their nuclear missiles from Cuba. The American media certainly saw the resolution of the crisis as a triumph for their President. Kennedy's Democratic Party colleagues reaped the reward with huge gains in elections against the Republicans ten days after the crisis.

However, Khrushchev could also claim some success. The United States had promised not to invade Cuba so the communist regime there was safe. He had also secured the withdrawal of American nuclear missiles from Italy and Turkey. Both of these were considerable gains in the circumstances. Castro's position in Cuba was strengthened as he knew that the Americans had agreed that Cuba would not be invaded by their forces. However, the deal to withdraw American missiles from Italy and Turkey was secret and Khrushchev could not brag about it. When Khrushchev was removed from power in 1964 one of the reasons was anger in the Soviet leadership at the concessions Khrushchev had made to the US as well as causing the crisis in the first place!

One other interesting point is that both sides showed considerable restraint during the crisis as each focused on the possible dangers of the escalation of events to a nuclear war. Both the United States and the Soviet Union realised that the weapons they had developed were a great threat to both sides. A third world war would be so destructive it was simply not worth it for the world. This led to a number of measures to limit nuclear weapons and improve communications between the two sides, which will be covered in Chapter 5.

Source 3.5

This was how one American cartoonist saw the result of the Cuban Missile Crisis. What evidence would support such a judgement? What evidence would oppose such a judgement?

BACKDOWN AT CASTRO GULCH

Interpretation and argument

Early explanations of Khrushchev's motives focused on the missiles as a way of expanding communism. Khrushchev was clear as to why there was an attempt to put nuclear missiles on Cuba. His memoirs focus on the desire to protect Cuba from American aggression and to threaten them with nuclear missiles as Russia was threatened by American missiles. To some extent these motives have been supported by the reminiscences of Soviet sources such as Oleg Troyanovsky, who was a special adviser to Khrushchev at the time of the crisis. John Gaddis also takes the view that the missile deployment was chiefly an effort to spread revolution throughout Latin America as well as a way of protecting Cuba from the Americans. Gaddis also feels that Khrushchev simply got carried away and did not think about the repercussions of his actions clearly as he was so emotionally committed to the Castro revolution. Gaddis goes so far as to describe Khrushchev as a 'petulant child' in terms of his behaviour.

The Cuban Missile Crisis of 1962

As to Kennedy's motives in standing up to Khrushchev, there has been a lively historical debate. To begin with, American views dominated any interpretation of the Cuban Missile Crisis. This is largely due to the publication of books by people such as Arthur Schlesinger who was a special assistant to John F. Kennedy and Bobby Kennedy. Such views emphasised the line that the placing of missiles in Cuba was to provoke the United States of America. Kennedy's response was interpreted as being appropriate and well-judged, and resulted in a triumph for American action. While this view is attractive from an American point of view, it takes a very partial view of the evidence as we now know.

Revisionist views emerged in the 1970s. Authors like T.G. Paterson were very critical of Kennedy's foreign policy, arguing that it was Kennedy's desire for personal and national prestige that were behind his response to the crisis. In particular, his awareness of a domestic need to appear strong over Cuba after the Bay of Pigs influenced him, as did awareness that domestic elections were coming up very soon. Others, such as M. White, point out that Kennedy's actions in allowing the Bay of Pigs contributed directly to Soviet actions in trying to place missiles on Cuba. Such views emphasise that the motivation for the placement of Soviet missiles was to protect vulnerable, communist Cuba rather than threaten America.

In recent years a more balanced view of the crisis has emerged of Kennedy's diplomacy and willingness to compromise, as shown by actions such as the decision to remove US missiles from Turkey.

Activities

How far can you go in answering these questions, using the information above?

Level 1: Can you select reasons why Batista's regime was unpopular in Cuba?

Level 2: Can you summarise the reasons for the failure of the Bay of Pigs?

Level 3: How would you show your understanding of Khrushchev's misjudgement of Kennedy?

Level 4: What is the relationship between the arms race and the Cuban Missile Crisis?

Level 5: What do you think were the main reasons for the Cuban Missile Crisis?

Level 6: What would you have done if faced with the same problems as President Kennedy faced with regard to Cuba?

3

Unit assessment practice

Complete a unit assessment standard:

> European and World Outcome 2 asks you to draw on and apply knowledge and understanding of complex European and World historical issues in a number of ways.

> Assessment standard 2.3 asks you to analyse a European and World historical issue.

Analyse the factors which were important in causing the Cuban Missile Crisis of 1962.

This may include:
- linking factors
- showing contradictions/inconsistencies between factors
- exploring different interpretations of these factors
- prioritising the factors.

For this exercise you will need to show understanding of at least two relevant factors as well as the above.

Extended response practice and Top Tip 3

Gaining marks for knowledge

This top tip provides advice on how to make sure you gain the maximum marks for knowledge.

The examples provided here all relate to the topic of this section which is: 'An evaluation of the reasons for the Cuban Missile Crisis of 1962.'

When you are preparing for the exam think very carefully about the style of question you will be asked and what the question will be about. In this case **all** the extended response questions will be about the issue mentioned above. In simple English the issue means – why was there a crisis involving the island of Cuba in 1962?

What sort of question will I be asked?

You should already know the four types of question that can be asked in Sections B or C of your exam paper which require an extended response answer. They are:

- To what extent ...
- How important ...
- A statement followed by 'How valid is this view?'
- How successfully ...

In this section you are asked to evaluate – or judge – what were the most important reasons why there was a crisis involving Cuba in 1962. There is

no one correct answer so a marker is looking for you to explain all the possible causes and then prioritise them by deciding which of the causes you think were more or less important than the others in causing the crisis. The important thing to do is make sure you have explained all the causes suggested within the illustrative areas for this topic before you make your final decision in response to the question.

Remember the question you are asked will be based closely on the title of this section and also on the illustrative areas. For this section the factors you should know about are:

- Castro's victory in Cuba
- US foreign policy
- Khrushchev's domestic position
- Kennedy's domestic context
- Khrushchev's view of Kennedy
- ideological differences
- the arms race
- mistakes by the leaders.

Likely questions on topic 3 are:

1 To what extent did Castro's victory in Cuba cause the Cuban Missile Crisis of 1962?

2 The arms race between the USA and USSR turned a revolution in a small island into an international crisis. How valid is this view?

3 How important was US foreign policy in causing the Cuban Missile Crisis of 1962?

The fourth type of question is 'How successfully … ?' but in a section that asks you to evaluate reasons why something happened, such as 'evaluate the reasons for the Cuban Missile Crisis of 1962' it is almost impossible to imagine a question that starts with 'How successfully … ?' These sorts of question are only used when the focus of the unit is on judging the effectiveness of something.

Knowledge

In any extended response there are 6 marks available for **relevant, detailed knowledge**, but you will not get 6 marks for simply mentioning a fact. For example, if someone wrote 'the President of the USA was John F. Kennedy' that person would NOT get a knowledge mark because the writer makes no attempt to link that information to the question, so it is not clearly relevant. If however the writer had written, 'The Cuban Missile Crisis was a test of willpower and strength for the leader of the Free World, US President John F. Kennedy' then that would get a mark because it fits in with the topic of the Cold War and the idea of a struggle involving the USA.

Nor will you get 6 marks for mentioning six small detailed facts that are linked to a major fact. For example, if you wrote, 'Cuba is an island (fact) in the Caribbean Sea (fact) which had a revolution in 1959 (fact). In that year Fidel Castro, supported by Che Guevara (fact), overthrew General Batista (fact)' you would not get 5 marks for knowledge, even though there are five facts in the short description of the Cuban revolution. Instead, you will only get one mark for writing about the Cuban revolution which was an important stage in leading to the international crisis in 1962. That is because your facts must be relevant to the question asked and not just fine detail based on the main fact. You *might* get 1 extra mark for detailed development of the point about the revolution, but that is all.

The easiest way to make sure you get 6 knowledge marks is to make sure you include at least three main facts which help to describe or explain important parts of your development of main factors. Put simply, if each main paragraph is about one of the factors you included in your introduction then try to include at least three important facts which help to develop (that means explain or describe) the factor.

For example, for the question, 'The arms race between the USA and USSR was the most important cause of the Cuban Missile Crisis. How valid is this view?' you would certainly have a paragraph about the arms race. That could include information about the USA's ability to reach the USSR with Jupiter missiles based in Turkey, Russia's inability to reach the USA with its own missiles and a third fact would be that missile bases in Cuba controlled by the USSR would bring US states and cities such as Florida, Texas and the capital city Washington D.C. within range of Soviet missiles. You can see there are three clearly separate facts in this development of the paragraph about the arms race. They are not the only facts you could include that would be relevant to a developed and relevant paragraph on the arms race but they give you an idea of what would gain 3 marks for knowledge. If you repeated this style of developing each main factor with several important facts then you will easily gain the full 6 marks for relevant Knowledge.

Here is a question for you to try yourself:

'Khrushchev's desire to win the arms race caused the Cuban Missile Crisis. How valid is this view?'

The Cuban Missile Crisis of 1962

The war in Vietnam

Vietnam is in Southeast Asia. It was here that the next major conflict of the Cold War would take place. Southeast Asia was a geographic area that American forces had already intervened in. Indeed, American troops were stationed in South Korea, propping up the anti-communist regime of Syngman Rhee, as the Vietnam crisis unfolded.

Indochina and the creation of Vietnam

Source 4.1

Explain why Southeast Asia was seen as an area that was under threat from the spread of communism?

The geographic area that now includes Vietnam and the surrounding countries of Laos and Cambodia had previously been called Indochina.

Indochina had been part of the colonial Empire established by the French in the nineteenth century. France had, however, been defeated by Germany in

1940 and its colonies in Indochina were occupied by the Japanese. Opposition to the Japanese grew with the emergence of an organisation called the Viet Minh, led by Ho Chi Minh. The Viet Minh was a communist-led nationalist movement which aimed to make Vietnam an independent country. They successfully defeated the Japanese occupation in 1945 and declared Vietnam independent.

Source 4.2

Ho Chi Minh (1890–1969) was one of the most important communist leaders of the twentieth century. He fought tirelessly for Vietnamese independence, but died in 1969 so did not witness the reunification of Vietnam in 1975.

However, after the end of the Second World War, the French planned to re-establish their colonial empire in Indochina and soon fighting between the French and Viet Minh broke out. The war between them lasted eight years and ended with the military defeat of the French in 1954 at the battle of Dien Bien Phu. This was an important event as one of the great colonial powers had been defeated militarily by local forces. Other colonial peoples across the world would take notice and learn how to oppose other colonial powers.

In 1954 the Geneva Agreements brought an end to the war between the French and Vietnamese, and France withdrew its forces from Indochina. Four new counties were created: Cambodia, Laos, North Vietnam and South Vietnam. Vietnam was to be split in two, but only for a short time. Elections were supposed to be held within two years, but in reality were never held.

Ho Chi Minh was not happy with the Geneva Agreements, as he was forced to give up the south of Vietnam. The two Vietnams developed very differently in the years after 1955. The North became a communist state under the leadership of Ho Chi Minh. Land was taken from private landowners and redistributed to the peasants. Health and education reforms were introduced. It was also a one party state where no opposition to the Communist Party was allowed. Much help was given to the North by

both communist China and the Soviet Union, though it is important to note that Vietnam was never a satellite state of the USSR.

The South, on the other hand, became a republic ruled by Ngo Dinh Diem. Diem had been placed into power by the Americans, who were seeking an anti-communist leader for South Vietnam. Diem had been in exile during the war with the French and thus was not tainted by association with them. Diem was also a Catholic, which the Americans hoped would make him reliable as an ally. However, Diem was authoritarian and ruled the country as a dictator. By the early 1960s his government had become an embarrassment to the Americans. Diem's family were appointed to important jobs and used their influence to enrich themselves. The majority of the population in South Vietnam were not Catholic and were treated badly as a result. Buddists, for example, were actively discriminated against. Opposition to Diem's rule grew as a result. There was no land reform in the South and no political freedom. In protest at the oppression of their faith, some Buddhist priests poured petrol over themselves, set it alight and were burned to death. Such images shocked the world. However, Diem simply responded to these crises with further violence. In 1960, the National Liberation Front (NLF) was formed to unite the opposition to Diem in South Vietnam. The NLF is more usually known as the Viet Cong. It was heavily influenced by the communist North.

America and growing involvement in Vietnam

America became increasingly concerned by what it saw as the further spread of communism across the world and in Southeast Asia in particular. President Eisenhower likened the spread of communism to a row of dominoes, saying:

> *You have a row of dominoes set up. You knock the first one and what will happen to the last one is a certainty, that it will go over very quickly.*

Source 4.3

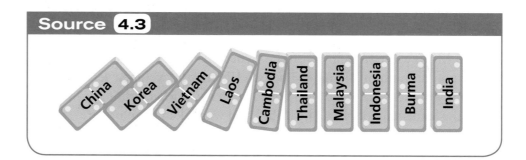

The theory was that if North Vietnam became communist so communism would spread to South Vietnam and then to Laos, Cambodia, Thailand, Burma and even India. Therefore, the logic was that communism had to be stopped in Vietnam. The Americans had misread the situation in a number of ways. In particular, they did not recognise that many of the freedom movements in Southeast Asia were nationalist in character, not simply communist.

The Americans were aware of the limitations of working with Diem, but they had few other options. Help was given to Diem's Government in the form of millions of dollars of aid and American advisers. While Diem was grateful for the aid, he did not listen to the advice of his American advisers to introduce land reform and to moderate his behaviour towards other religious groups.

When Kennedy became President in 1961 he was occupied by events in Cuba and Berlin. However, Vietnam continued to be a concern for the Americans, particularly the growth in attacks on Diem and his supporters. Kennedy resisted sending in ground troops, but the number of military advisers was increased to 3000 and America hoped that Diem would accept the need for reforms. However, the security situation continued to deteriorate and by 1962 American pilots were flying combat missions in Vietnam. The numbers of American military personnel in Vietnam had increased to 11,500 by the end of 1962. By 1963, Diem was cracking down on the Buddhist population of South Vietnam once again. This was the final shraw for America. Encouraged by the CIA, a group of South Vietnamese generals overthrew Diem's regime. Diem and his brother Nhu were murdered. Kennedy was horrified.

The Americans had given little thought as to what to do after the removal of Diem. The situation was further complicated when, three weeks later, President Kennedy was assassinated, shot during a visit to Dallas. Kennedy was succeeded by his Vice President, Lyndon B. Johnson, who then won a convincing victory in the 1964 Presidential election.

Source 4.4

Lyndon Baines Johnson (1908–73) was President of the United States between 1963 and 1969. He had been Vice President, but succeeded as President on the death of John F. Kennedy. He won the Presidential election of 1964, but did not seek re-election in 1968.

Johnson firmly believed that the Soviet Union and communist China were behind the growing number of attacks made in South Vietnam. He believed that communism's spread must be stopped. Therefore, Johnson gave permission for a large military escalation by the Americans in South Vietnam. In this he was backed by the American Congress. By the end of 1963 there were 20,000 American military personnel in Vietnam. This number rapidly increased still further.

After the death of Diem a series of military governments tried to control South Vietnam. Few survived long. This created a power vacuum in the South as the credibility of the South Vietnamese Government simply did not exist. At the same time the communist threat developed. By the mid-1960s large areas of South Vietnam were in the control of the guerrilla fighters of the Viet Cong.

The military situation deteriorated further. In 1962, under American guidance, South Vietnamese troops had moved many peasants into fortified villages called 'strategic hamlets'. The basic idea was that the strategic hamlets would improve security in the countryside and protect peasants against guerrilla attacks by the Viet Cong. However, such a policy was understandably unpopular with the peasants and it turned many into supporters of the Viet Cong. The fortified villages also proved to be of limited value. Of the 3000 created, around 2000 had been destroyed by the Viet Cong by the end of 1963. By 1965, up to 60,000 communist guerrilla soldiers were operating in the South. They were supplied by a supply line that went from North Vietnam through the jungles of Laos and Cambodia and into South Vietnam. This was known as the Ho Chi Minh Trail.

In 1964, events in the Gulf of Tonkin allowed for more direct military escalation by the United States. The US destroyer *Maddox* was fired at by North Vietnamese gunboats as it gathered information in the Gulf of Tonkin off the coast of North Vietnam. A second attack allegedly took place two days later. This second attack never happened, but Johnson used this as evidence of an unprovoked attack by the North on the United States. He demanded a response. The result of this was the Gulf of Tonkin Resolution, which was passed by the US Congress in 1964. This gave Johnson the power to send military supplies and combat troops into Vietnam. At the time opinion polls in the United States showed 85 per cent support for government actions. However, it is interesting to note that there was never a formal declaration of war by the American Government on North Vietnam, which allowed people to question the legality of the war and the way it was prosecuted.

In 1964 Johnson won the Presidential election by a massive majority. He promised to build a 'Great Society' in the United States and actively oppose

communism in Southeast Asia. American military commitment to the
conflict in Vietnam started to increase. Between 1964 and 1968 massive
resources were built up in South Vietnam. The first US marines landed in
1965. By the end of that year there were 183,000 American troops in
Vietnam. By the end of 1968 this number had increased to 535,000. In
total, between 1965 and 1973, just over 1.6 million Americans fought in
Vietnam. Of these, 58,202 died and 303,704 were injured. Over 2 million
Vietnamese lost their lives.

American military plans and problems

Operation Rolling Thunder

The American military strategy was based around the aerial bombardment of
North Vietnam and defeating the Viet Cong within South Vietnam. The US
launched Operation Rolling Thunder in 1965 after a series of Viet Cong
attacks on US military installations. Operation Rolling Thunder allowed for
giant American B-52 aircraft to pour bombs down on North Vietnam. It
lasted for eight long years and totally failed in its objective of bringing the
North Vietnamese to the negotiating table. There were a number of reasons
for this. Firstly, North Vietnam was a largely agricultural country with a lot of
jungle cover. It was difficult to target specific military and industrial targets,
and there was not a lot of infrastructure for the Americans to target. For
example, they hoped that mass bombing would disrupt supplies coming down
the Ho Chi Minh Trail. However, this totally failed. Any damage was rapidly
fixed and supplies were transported by bicycle or on the backs of porters.

To try to deal with the dense jungle cover that hid the North Vietnamese
Army and the Viet Cong, the Americans dropped 18 million gallons of
herbicides. One particularly nasty chemical defoliant used was known as
Agent Orange. In total the United States dropped more bombs on Vietnam
than were dropped by all combatant nations during the Second World War.
The American bombing effort caused huge destruction and loss of life, but
in reality had little effect on the North Vietnamese war effort.

Foreign aid to the North Vietnamese and Viet Cong

One reason for the strength of the North Vietnamese war effort was the
equipment and training given to them by the Soviet Union and China. This
military help enabled the North Vietnamese to defend themselves
effectively. The Soviet Union supplied MiG fighter aircraft and anti-aircraft
guns which allowed the North Vietnamese to shoot down 700 American
planes. Their military assistance also allowed the Viet Cong to increase
their attacks in the South.

The war in Vietnam

Strengths of the Viet Cong

The Viet Cong was a guerrilla army. They did not wear uniforms and blended in well with the local peasant population. They set traps for the US and South Vietnamese soldiers and used hit-and-run tactics. On the other hand, the American military was highly trained but this training was aimed at fighting a conventional war in Europe. As a result, they found it difficult to distinguish between a South Vietnamese civilian and a Viet Cong soldier.

The American answer to guerrilla warfare in Vietnam was air mobility. They put together a huge airmobile effort. For example, the 1st Aviation Brigade, established in May 1966, contained 24,000 men and 4230 aircraft. These mobile units would launch search and destroy operations. Firstly, possible enemy units were identified. Air support and artillery would soften up the target with high explosive or napalm (fire bombs). Then troop-carrying helicopters, supported by helicopter gunships, would sweep in and deploy ground troops. Helicopters allowed for the swift removal of casualties and the addition of reinforcements.

These tactics had limited success against guerrilla fighters like the Viet Cong. Large numbers of innocent South Vietnamese were killed in these strikes and the Viet Cong also proved able to punish the Americans. Almost 5000 helicopters were lost during the war. Each helicopter cost a quarter of a million dollars. The US also lost nearly 6000 pilots and crew. This made up around one tenth of US deaths during the war.

Source 4.5

American power in action. Why was such power often ineffective in the Vietnam War?

Difficulties faced by the US soldiers

One of the biggest problems for the Americans was the nature of jungle war. The terrain was difficult to cover and it was hot. It was relatively easy for the enemy to hide and this lead to fear of the hit-and-run attacks in which the Viet Cong specialised. Jungle warfare ground down American troops' morale. Furthermore, morale was not helped by the fact that American equipment was often inferior to that used by the Viet Cong. For example, the standard infantry weapon used by US troops was the M-16 assault rifle. It was not suited to jungle warfare as it frequently jammed. In contrast, the Viet Cong used the robust AK-47. Then there was the use of booby traps or mines by the Viet Cong. These caused 11 per cent of US combat deaths between 1965 and 1970. Traps were often as simple as sharpened bamboo stakes smeared with human excrement, hidden in pits. Such weapons created great fear among US troops and further lowered morale.

The problem of South Vietnam

Even well-motivated troops found that their beliefs were tested by the reality of Vietnam. Many Americans felt that they were fighting to defend a free democracy. However, the reality was that South Vietnam was a corrupt military dictatorship. By 1965, General Thieu was Head of State and Ky Air-Vice Marshal Nguyen Cao was Prime Minister. Thieu was a corrupt, indecisive womaniser who drank and gambled. Ky liked to be seen in dark glasses, carrying pearl-handled revolvers. Both men were unpopular with ordinary South Vietnamese. They commanded a divided military force. Most officers in the South Vietnamese Army were Catholic and from the landowning class while the ordinary soldiers were peasants. Different South Vietnamese army groups operated as little more than private armies for their generals. Many of the generals were corrupt.

Co-ordinated attacks on the Viet Cong and North Vietnamese Army did not happen. The Americans ran 'Search and Destroy' missions; they joked that the South Vietnamese Army went on 'Search and Avoid' missions. Defending a corrupt regime with a poorly motivated military did not go down well with the ordinary American soldier. Many simply fought to stay alive. One popular saying was to 'CYA (cover your ass) and get home'. American soldiers took to painting UUUU on their helmets: 'the unwilling, led by the unqualified, doing the unnecessary, for the ungrateful'. Drug use by US soldiers became a problem, with widespread use of marijuana and heroin. As the war went on, respect for officers also declined. There were instances of 'fragging', where officers were killed by their own troops. At least 83 American officers were killed in this way.

Winning hearts and minds?

American soldiers had little in common with the ordinary South Vietnamese peasant. They did not speak the same language and did not understand the culture. Racism became common, with terms like 'gooks' used to describe the ordinary Vietnamese. The de-humanising of the local population led to atrocities. The most famous example is the massacre of 350 unarmed civilians in the Vietnamese village of My Lai by American troops. The American commander, Lieutenant William Calley, stated that:

 I was ordered to go in there and destroy the enemy. That was my job … that was the mission I was given. I did not sit down and think in terms of men, women and children. They were all classified the same. … I felt then and I still do that I acted as I was directed, and I carried out the orders that I was given and I do not feel wrong in doing so …

Such behaviour, coupled with the deaths of many innocent South Vietnamese by American bombing, as well as the destruction of their crops by defoliants like Agent Orange, meant that the Americans lost the battle for the 'hearts and minds' of the local population. Many South Vietnamese were also forced to move from their land into controlled strategic hamlets or urban centres. There were American civilian 'experts' who tried to help the South Vietnamese with building, but the Americans tended to think of the war in purely military terms.

North Vietnam and its strengths

The North Vietnamese were well led by decisive and determined figures like Ho Chi Minh and General Giap. Ho Chi Minh had led his people to victory over the Japanese, French and now the Americans. The figure of 'Uncle Ho' was very popular. The main military leader of the North Vietnamese was General Giap. He recognised that the Vietnamese would suffer many more casualties than the Americans, but also knew that they had the determination and motivation to take the casualties as they were fighting for a cause they believed in. In contrast to the United States soldiers, the Viet Cong signed up for a life of fighting instead of the one-year draft. The Viet Cong were also strictly controlled regarding their behaviour. When operating in the South they were told to be polite to villagers, not steal food or flirt with the women. In areas they controlled, land reform took place, with land given to the ordinary peasants. This had great appeal to the Southern population.

Source 4.6

Viet Cong soldiers. Why did fighting in civilian clothes give the Viet Cong an advantage?

The Tet Offensive and growing public opposition to the war

Tet is the Vietnamese New Year. It was the most important festival in the Vietnamese calendar. In January 1968 the Viet Cong and North Vietnamese Army, or the NVA (also known as the People's Army of Vietnam or ARVN), chose Tet to launch a surprise attack across South Vietnam. The North Vietnamese Army launched probing attacks across the border with South Vietnam, and the Viet Cong launched assaults within the heart of South Vietnam. They hoped that the attack would encourage a general rising against the South Vietnamese Government by the population. Other aims were to destabilise the South Vietnamese Army and show the vulnerability of the Americans. Over one hundred attacks were launched comprising roughly 60,000 North Vietnamese regular soldiers and Viet Cong. Almost every military and political target of importance in South Vietnam was attacked. In Saigon a Viet Cong commando unit even managed to enter the US Embassy compound. Images of American troops fighting in their own Embassy were caught on camera. War had been brought to the towns and cities of South Vietnam in the most brutal and direct way. Americans and the world were shocked by what they saw.

In reality, Tet was a military disaster for the Viet Cong and the ARVN. Both suffered heavy losses. The ARVN was driven back and the Viet Cong lost some of its best fighters in the offensive. The South also failed to rise up against their government, although the South Vietnamese Army did suffer casualties and desertion rates increased. The Americans also suffered casualties. Many cities had been devastated as the Americans and South Vietnamese used massive firepower to remove the enemy, and the South Vietnamese Government was under increased pressure owing to the huge increase in numbers of refugees as a result of the offensive. Money and resources would have to be used to feed and house this population. As they recovered cities, such as the city of Hue, they uncovered the execution of government officials and anyone else who was seen as being pro-South Vietnam Government. However, the importance of Tet in terms of America's defeat was in how it was seen in America. There were particularly important consequences over how Tet was interpreted in the United States.

Interpretation of the Tet Offensive

The American media had considerable influence on public opinion back home. A lot of what was said about Tet was not true, but back home in America it had an impact. General Westmoreland gave press conferences regarding the attack, emphasising the ability of the Americans and their South Vietnamese allies to repel it. He assured reporters that everything was going well. However, the reporters based in Saigon told a different story. A lot of this was to do with what they thought they knew. They heard the Viet Cong attack on the American Embassy and assumed that the Viet Cong had penetrated the embassy and were in control of its lower floors. In fact the embassy remained sealed to the enemy, but that did not stop the newspaper interpretation of events. For example, on 2 February the respected *New York Times* reported that Viet Cong guerrillas had occupied the first floor of the American Embassy. They followed with an opinion piece that the Tet Offensive was a success for the enemy and threw into doubt government claims that the war was being won. Other newspapers and television commentators supported such claims.

The daily flow of information coming back from Vietnam seemed to confirm this line. The war in Vietnam was a television war, one which was widely reported back home in America. The American public had been told that they were winning the war. However, a growing number of body bags and returning wounded soldiers were telling a different story. The images of the Tet Offensive showed that the Viet Cong could strike at the very heart of America's presence in Vietnam. Events during Tet also showed that Americans' hopes of a quick victory were false. The horror of American behaviour, such as the My Lai Massacre, and use of horrific weapons, like napalm, were also reported. The following image of Vietnamese civilians fleeing a napalm attack is a good example of the real-life stories that news outlets reported.

Source 4.7

The perception was that, despite the promises made by the US military, the war was not being won. It was also increasingly difficult to see the Americans as the 'good guys'. By March 1968 a Gallup poll revealed that 69 per cent of Americans favoured a phased withdrawal of American troops from Vietnam once local forces had been trained up.

Opposition to the war had been growing in America since 1966. The public face of this was through massive public protest marches. In October 1967 between 50,000 and 100,000 protesters against the war marched through Washington D.C. In the autumn of 1969 over 250,000 demonstrated against the war. There were also widespread protests on many university campuses. This led to confrontation. At Kent State University in Ohio, National Guardsmen opened fire on student protesters, killing four. Violence erupted across America's universities.

Ordinary Americans resisted military call-up (called 'the draft') by publicly burning their call-up letters. Up to a quarter of a million young Americans did this, many chanting, 'Hell no, we won't go!' as they did so.

Source 4.8

This is a famous photograph of Jeffrey Miller minutes after he was shot dead by the Ohio National Guard. Why was such a photograph front-page news in the USA?

The war was also increasingly expensive: it was costing $2000 million a month by 1968. This meant there was little money to fund President Johnson's plans to build a 'Great Society' in the United States. There were also economic problems as the costs of financing the war placed a great strain on the American economy. Those people who loaned the Americans money, such as European bankers, increasingly withdrew their money from America when they could. America was looking like a risky investment in light of its large expenditure on a war that it did not appear to be winning. Some people began to question the point of the conflict as a result. Importantly, politicians, even those that supported the war, increasingly wanted to control and limit American involvement. When General Westmoreland asked for yet more soldiers in response to the Tet Offensive, the politicians refused as it was seen as being 'politically impossible'.

Johnson was increasingly criticised about how the war was being conducted and on his leadership (or lack of it). Common chants that confronted him wherever he went included, 'Hey, hey LBJ; how many kids did you kill today?' In a democracy, public opinion and public support for government actions matter. It is important to remember, however, that there was still significant support for the war among sections of the American population. Though vocal, the anti-war movement did have limits. Even in 1968, Gallup polls showed that 71 per cent of respondents favoured bombing North Vietnam. Anti-war protesters were attacked by 'patriots'. For example, on 8 May 1970 over two hundred hard-hat construction workers attacked a crowd of anti-war protesters. Supporters of the war,

Extended response practice and Top Tip 4

This top tip provides advice on how to make sure you gain the maximum marks for basic analysis and 'analysis plus' marks. Within the total marks available for your extended response (that is your essay) you can gain 4 marks for basic analysis and an extra 2 marks for analysis plus.

The examples provided here all relate to Section 4 of the Cold War, 1945 which is 'An evaluation of the reasons why the US lost the war in Vietnam.'

Please **do not** worry about evaluation marks in this section. Evaluation marks are part of Top Tip 5.

In this section you are asked to evaluate – or judge – what were the most important reasons why the USA lost the Vietnam War. There is no one correct answer so a marker is looking for you to explain all the possible causes and then prioritise them by deciding which of the causes you think were more or less important than the others in causing America's defeat. The important thing to do is make sure you have explained all the causes suggested within the illustrative areas for this topic before you make your final decision in response to the question.

When you are preparing for the exam think very carefully about the style of question you will be asked and what the question will be about. In this case **all** the extended response questions will be about the issue mentioned above. In simple English the issue means – why did the USA lose the Vietnam War?

What sort of question will I be asked?

You should already know the types of extended response question that can be asked so remind yourself how the following words form part of the three types of questions. The words are: **extent, valid, important**. The word 'successfully' is not so likely to crop up in a question for this section because it is not easy to write about how successful something was when you are looking at reasons why something happened. Try it yourself. Make up three questions relevant to this section, with each question using one of the bold words from the list above. Then look at the illustrative examples for this section below and then try to write a 'How successfully ... ?' question linked to why America lost the Vietnam War. You will find that last task very difficult which is why you are unlikely to get a 'How successfully ... ?' question in this section.

Likely questions on Topic 4 are:

1 To what extent was changing public opinion in the USA the main reason why the USA lost the war in Vietnam?

2 The Vietnam war was lost because of military difficulties faced by the USA. How valid is this view?

3 How important were the relative strengths of North and South Vietnam in causing the US defeat in Vietnam?

How do I get good marks for basic analysis?

All the examples here apply to content from Section 4 of the Cold War which is about the Vietnam War.

There are 4 marks available for basic analysis and an extra 2 marks for developed analysis. To get the marks available you should aim to do two things:

The first is to make a straightforward comment on the importance of your information in terms of what the question is about. For example, in a question about why America lost the Vietnam War, if you include some factual information about American anti-war public opinion during the war such as: 'Many young American men burned their draft cards rather than go and fight in the war', then you may gain a knowledge mark. However, you can easily get a basic analysis mark by adding the word 'because' then giving a reason why anti-war public opinion became an important reason for US defeat.

You could write something like this: 'Many young American men burned their draft cards rather than go and fight in the war. This was important because it showed to the world and to the North Vietnamese that many Americans were against the war and that America was losing the willpower to keep fighting.' This shows how a basic analysis comment can be linked to information you have included.

The comment is basic analysis because it is relevant to the subject of the question but it does not focus on the issue, which means it does not try to answer the 'To what extent' or 'How important' or 'How valid' part of the question. However, a basic analysis has been made.

Remember! To get a basic analysis comment mark you must make a simple comment that links to the subject of the question you are answering. Do it four times in your extended response and you can get up to 4 marks.

How do I gain extra marks for developed analysis?

If you use developed analysis you can gain up to a maximum of 6 marks. This would be an additional 2 marks to your four relevant basic analysis points.

There are many ways to be given developed analysis marks. You can gain marks by comparing factors (this factor was successful, while this factor led to ...) or through counter arguments (However ...).

In your introduction you included 'factors to develop'. In this topic on why America lost the Vietnam War the factors provided for you by the SQA are:

- difficulties faced by the US military
- relative strengths of North and South Vietnam
- failure of military methods
- changing public opinion in the USA
- international isolation of the USA.

Assuming your extended responses are properly organised with separate paragraphs dealing with each factor, to get a developed analysis mark your comments must link to the factor you are writing about and not just generally to the topic of the essay.

For example, if you were writing about the failure of US bombing to close the Ho Chi Minh Trail (which is a Knowledge point) and you wrote: 'America's attempt to stop supply routes between North Vietnam and South Vietnam failed and this was important because it meant the Viet Cong in the South could be supplied with equipment to launch attacks in the South and weaken US morale', you will get a basic analysis mark because what you wrote is true but it only linked to the overall topic of the essay.

To get developed analysis marks, more focus is needed on the factor you are writing about, which in this case is 'difficulties faced by the US military'. You should therefore try to write something like: 'America's attempt to stop supply routes between North Vietnam and South Vietnam by extensive bombing of the Ho Chi Minh Trail failed and this was important because it demonstrated the failure of US military methods and illustrated a main reason why the USA lost the Vietnam war.'

Another possible question on Section 4 of the Cold War topic is:

How important were the strengths of North Vietnam as a reason for the American defeat in the Vietnam War?

4

Attempts to control the Cold War

Throughout the Cold War period there were efforts by both sides to resolve problems. In order to do this, processes were developed to maintain contact between the two sides. Serious efforts were also being made to reduce the amount of armaments both sides had. There are a number of reasons why this happened.

The theory of mutual assured destruction

Both superpowers developed huge arsenals of nuclear weaponry in the 1950s and 1960s. What follows is a timeline giving the main stages and events in the developing arms race.

Source 5.1

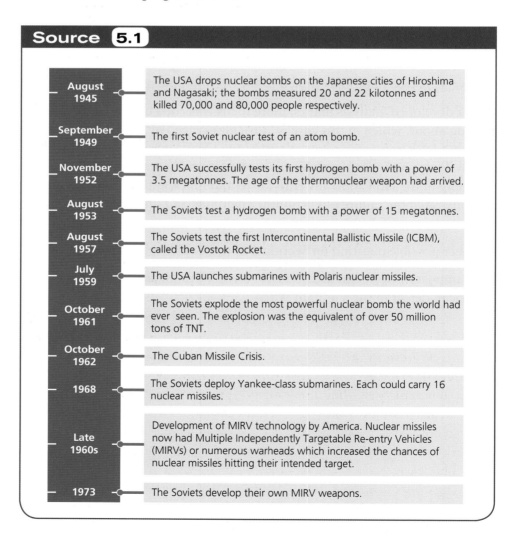

August 1945	The USA drops nuclear bombs on the Japanese cities of Hiroshima and Nagasaki; the bombs measured 20 and 22 kilotonnes and killed 70,000 and 80,000 people respectively.
September 1949	The first Soviet nuclear test of an atom bomb.
November 1952	The USA successfully tests its first hydrogen bomb with a power of 3.5 megatonnes. The age of the thermonuclear weapon had arrived.
August 1953	The Soviets test a hydrogen bomb with a power of 15 megatonnes.
August 1957	The Soviets test the first Intercontinental Ballistic Missile (ICBM), called the Vostok Rocket.
July 1959	The USA launches submarines with Polaris nuclear missiles.
October 1961	The Soviets explode the most powerful nuclear bomb the world had ever seen. The explosion was the equivalent of over 50 million tons of TNT.
October 1962	The Cuban Missile Crisis.
1968	The Soviets deploy Yankee-class submarines. Each could carry 16 nuclear missiles.
Late 1960s	Development of MIRV technology by America. Nuclear missiles now had Multiple Independently Targetable Re-entry Vehicles (MIRVs) or numerous warheads which increased the chances of nuclear missiles hitting their intended target.
1973	The Soviets develop their own MIRV weapons.

side could build to two each. An interim agreement set a five-year freeze on US and Soviet missile launchers at their existing levels. Limits were placed on the number of ICBMs (Intercontinental Ballistic Missiles) – 1,054 for the USA and 1,618 for the Soviets – and SLBMs (Submarine Launched Ballistic Missiles) – 656 for the USA and 740 for the Soviets. Note that this was limiting the number of launchers, *not* warheads . As the US had multiple warheads for their missiles they were willing to allow the Soviets more launchers. There was a mad logic at work here. Both sides were effectively determining how they could guarantee the destruction of the other side, even at the point when they are being destroyed themselves. In effect, the treaty would guarantee the destruction of the world. Assured destruction and deterrence were now secured in treaty form.

SALT I was a small, but important step. However, future agreements proved to be difficult owing to improvements in technology. In 1973 the Soviets developed their own MIRV (Multiple Independently Targetable Re-entry Vehicle) systems. Both sides improved their existing technology and developed Intermediate Nuclear weapons which had a shorter flight time to their targets, therefore giving both sides much less time to decide on their response. In the case of America, this meant the development of Pershing and Cruise missiles. The Soviets developed their SS-20 missile. Talks did go ahead from 1977 to 1979 and a SALT II Treaty was signed in Vienna by Presidents Carter and Brezhnev. The Treaty sought to limit launchers of all kinds as well as place limits on the numbers of MIRV warheads that could be deployed. However, it was never ratified by the US Senate and when the Soviet Union invaded Afghanistan in 1979 détente stopped. In 1980 the US Senate rejected SALT II. Arms Control only returned when Mikhail Gorbachev became Soviet Leader in 1985.

Development of surveillance technology

The idea of open inspection of each other's missile sites was opposed by the military leaders of both sides. However, as technology improved, other ways of making sure each side was sticking to its treaty commitments was developed.

In September 1946, the United States conducted the first of many intelligence-gathering missions against the Soviets. It used a converted jet bomber that was carrying surveillance cameras instead of bombs. As the Cold War progressed, the Americans developed specialist spy planes, such as the Lockheed U-2. These aircraft could fly fast and at a high altitude. They also contained increasingly sophisticated cameras. During the Korean War, allied forces collected hundreds of thousands of images and flew an average of 2,000 surveillance missions a month throughout the war.

Source 5.5

A U-2 spy plane.

Overflights of Cuba by U-2 spy aircraft provided the intelligence that was critical to the discovery that the Soviets were planning to deploy nuclear weapons on the island. They would also be used to verify that the nuclear installations were being dismantled at the end of the crisis.

Beginning in 1969, aerial surveillance helped in the search for peace as it provided intelligence that helped US diplomats taking part in the Strategic Arms Limitation Talks. Throughout the era of détente that opened with these arms limitation talks, the United States continued to conduct surveillance against the Soviet Union as the Soviet Union did against the United States. Surveillance offered both sides a chance to verify what the other was doing. However, as we have seen, it did not stop the development of increasingly sophisticated nuclear weapons by both sides.

Interpretation and argument

There is considerable disagreement about whether controlling the Cold War through détente was a good thing or not. On one side are historians who see détente as being of great benefit as it made the world a safer place. American politicians like Henry Kissinger, who were heavily involved in détente, and historians like G. Craig support this view. Ranged against this view are those who think that attempts to control the Cold War were weak and allowed communism to continue. Historians like R. Pipes support this view. They tend to be very critical of President Carter and feel that détente was bound to fail as the USSR was communist and expansionist. They look at the Soviet invasion of Afghanistan in 1979 and the eventual collapse of communism as evidence to support their view.

Activities

Create a fishbone diagram to explain in detail why the superpowers tried to control the Cold War:

- Work in small groups to produce a poster explaining why the superpowers tried to control the Cold War.

- Your teacher will give you a template with the key question: 'Why did the superpowers try to control the Cold War?' at the top. The template will give the outline of a fish skeleton.

- Each group should place the effect – 'Made the superpowers control the Cold War' at the tip, or nose, of the skeleton.

- The bold lines (or fish bones) represent possible main causes. The smaller horizontal 'bones' add further detail to the main bones. Some causes have been filled in already.

- Each group should complete the fishbone diagram.

- Debrief: each group member should be able to explain, in detail, at least one reason why the superpowers tried to control the Cold War.

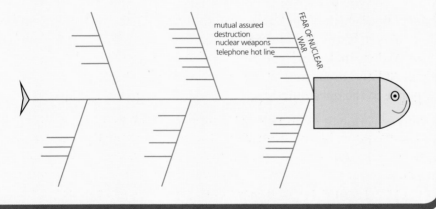

mutual assured destruction
nuclear weapons
telephone hot line
FEAR OF NUCLEAR WAR

Unit assessment practice

Complete a unit assessment standard:

European and World Outcome 2 asks you to draw on and apply knowledge and understanding of complex European and World historical issues in a number of ways.

Assessment standard 2.2 asks you to explain, with accuracy, a European and World historical issue.

An example might be:

Explain the reasons why the superpowers tried to control the Cold War.

Extended response practice and Top Tip 5: How to gain evaluation marks

This top tip provides advice on how to gain up to four **evaluation** marks.

Within the total marks available for your extended response (essay) you can gain 4 marks for evaluation.

The examples provided here all relate to Section 5 of the Cold War, 1945–89 which is: 'An evaluation of the reasons why the superpowers attempted to manage the Cold War, 1962–85.'

What sort of question will I be asked?

In this section you are asked to evaluate – or judge – the reasons why the USSR and the USA 'attempted to manage' the Cold War. This is another way of asking why the superpowers USA and USSR took steps after the early 1960s to reduce the risk that a localised conflict such as Cuba could have escalated into a major nuclear war that could have 'mutually assured' the destruction of each other.

There is no one correct answer which explains why the superpowers tried to make sure the Cold War did not explode into a hot conflict so a marker is looking for you to explain all the possible causes and then prioritise them by deciding which of the causes you think were more or less important than the others in leading to attempts to manage the Cold War. The important thing to do is make sure you have explained all the causes suggested within the illustrative areas for this topic before you make your final decision in response to the question.

Just like Sections 1, 3 and 4, in this topic it is almost impossible to imagine a question that starts with 'How successfully … ?' These sorts of question are only used when the focus of the unit is on judging the effectiveness of something.

Possible questions on Topic 5 are:

1 To what extent was the danger of mutual assured destruction the main reason why the superpowers attempted to manage the Cold War between 1962 and 1985?

2 The ever increasing cost of the arms race meant that attempts to manage the Cold War were inevitable. How valid is this view?

3 How important was the development of surveillance technology in pushing the superpowers towards coexistence and détente?

How do I get evaluation marks on top of my analysis marks?

Evaluation is the judgement you make about the relative importance of the various **factors** in terms of the question rather than just commenting on the factual details you include about each individual factor.

The **factors** to develop are, of course, the factors which you included in your introduction. In this section on the reasons why the superpowers attempted

to manage the Cold War. The factors are once again provided for you by the SQA under the heading 'Illustrative examples'. These are:

1 the danger of mutual assured destruction

2 the dangers of military conflict as seen in the Cuban Missile Crisis

3 the economic cost of the arms race

4 the development of surveillance technology

5 policies of coexistence and détente.

The phrase used on page 92 – 'in terms of the question' – is really important for evaluation marks because you are not just writing about a topic. You must focus your judgement on exactly what the question is asking you. For example, you could make an overall judgement, with reasons of course, that the move towards greater détente was the result of the economic cost of the arms race rather than the softening of the opposing ideological views of the superpowers. In fact, that overall judgement shows a fairly straightforward way of adding evaluation to your extended response by basing your answer around the illustrative examples in the SQA syllabus for this section and prioritising them in order of importance.

There is, of course, no absolute correct order of importance but if you can argue a case **with reasons** that one factor was more important than another then you are evaluating!

Yet another route to evaluation marks is to refer to the opinions of different writers on the subject. Show your awareness of the different opinions and make a decision yourself about which of the opinions you agree with most. A straightforward way of gaining evaluation marks in this manner is to present your set of conflicting opinions like this:

'Of course there are different opinions about why the superpowers moved closer to détente and coexistence. While Simon Wood in his book *The Cold War 1945–1985* argues that the cost of the arms race was the central reason why the superpowers became more co-operative, Green in his analysis of Cold War developments argues that the fear of mutual assured destruction was the most important factor influencing superpower foreign policy.'

1–2 marks can be awarded for isolated evaluative comments used as a direct answer to the main question but 3–4 marks can be awarded where the candidate connects the evaluative comments together and links them to the line of argument outlined in the introduction.

Another possible question on Section 5 of the Cold War topic is:

'To what extent can the superpowers' attempts to control the Cold War be explained by fear of mutual assured destruction?'

The end of the Cold War

By the late 1970s the era of détente was coming to an end. Events in Afghanistan, Poland and within the Soviet Union itself would put huge pressure on the communist governments in Eastern Europe. The election of a new American President who was willing to challenge communist rule was also a factor, as was the emergence of a new Soviet leadership that saw the need for communism to reform. The collapse of communism in Eastern Europe, by 1989, and then the Soviet Union, in 1991, was unexpected at the time. Today we know that underlying pressures on the Soviet economy as well as poor military decisions led to attempts to reform communism. These attempts proved futile as the restless peoples of Eastern Europe freed themselves from the restrictions of communism.

The end of détente

Source 6.1

All the countries in colour were once part of the Soviet Union. You can see how Russia dominated.

SWEDEN
GERMANY
CZECH REPUBLIC
LITHUANIA FINLAND
Barents Sea
Kara Sea
POLAND
ESTONIA
LATVIA
SLOVAKIA
BELARUS
HUNGARY
ROMANIA
MOLDOVA
UKRAINE
RUSSIA
Black Sea
AZERBAIJAN
GEORGIA
TURKEY
SYRIA
KAZAKHSTAN
Caspian Sea
MONGOLIA
IRAQ
UZBEKISTAN
KUWAIT ARMENIA
TURKMENISTAN
KYRGYZSTAN
IRAN
TAJIKISTAN
CHINA
SAUDIA ARABIA
Parsian Gulf
AFGHANISTAN
PAKISTAN

Defence Initiative. In the end only disagreements over Reagan's Star Wars programme stopped an agreement being signed. However, both sides now knew that there was a will to reduce the threat of nuclear war.

In 1987, Gorbachev agreed to the removal of all Soviet and US intermediate nuclear forces in Europe. The INF Treaty was signed in December 1987. It did away with a whole class of nuclear weapons: Soviet SS-20 missiles and US Pershing and Cruise missiles would be dismantled and removed from Europe. It was the most comprehensive and open treaty so far. Both sides agreed to open verification of their actions. Such acts built up trust between the sides and allowed for more agreements to be made.

Then, in 1988, Gorbachev went even further. He announced massive reductions in conventional Soviet military forces by promising to cut 500,000 troops. This included the removal of huge numbers of tanks, aircraft and artillery from Eastern Europe. He also, importantly, stated that the Soviet satellite states were freed from Soviet control and could choose their own futures. Soviet troops would no longer enforce communism in Eastern Europe. It must be remembered that Gorbachev wanted a reformed communism. He certainly did not want it to end. However, the unpopularity of communism as a political force soon became clear. The fact that the Soviet forces would not intervene to save communism no doubt played an important role later. All of a sudden the old order was gone. The people of Eastern Europe would now act.

The collapse of communism in the Soviet satellite states

The first country to taste greater freedom was Hungary. The old leader János Kádár was forced to retire in 1988 and a new Prime Minister, Miklós Németh came to power. His government recognised that the 1956 uprising had been a genuinely popular event. Imre Nagy, the Hungarian leader who had led the rebellion and was killed on the orders of Khrushchev, was reburied. The funeral was watched by 200,000 Hungarians. Hungarian guards were ordered to dismantle the barbed-wire fence along the border with Austria. The Soviet Union did not object and other countries in the Warsaw Pact took notice.

Communism as a political force was defeated in Poland by 1989. In 1988, Solidarity was legalised and free elections were allowed. In 1989, Solidarity won a landslide victory and the Communist Party collapsed. The Soviet Union did nothing, with Gorbachev stating that this was a matter to be decided by Poland. Soon other communist states were also in trouble. In Czechoslovakia a leading opponent of communism, Václav Havel, was elected President in 1989.

East Germany has always been an artificial country. Many East Germans had taken advantage of the opening of the Hungarian border by travelling there to go on holiday and then walking across the border to claim asylum. By 1989, mass demonstrations in the streets increased the pressure for reform. Rather than crushing the protests with force, the East German Government decided to open access to the Berlin Wall. In the event, on 9 November 1989 sections of the wall were smashed down. A massive symbol of communist power and control had been broken. East Germany oversaw free elections in 1990 that returned political parties in favour of the reunification of Germany. Gorbachev eventually accepted the reality of a reunited Germany and its future membership of NATO. The great symbol of the divide between the capitalist West and communist East was breached. By the end of 1989, every pro-Soviet communist government in Eastern Europe had ceased to exist.

Source 6.7

The Berlin Wall is smashed down. Why was the Wall such an important symbol of the Cold War?

The collapse of communism in the East European states is seen by many historians as the end of the Cold War. The symbolic destruction of the Berlin Wall and the ending of one-party rule in the East European states certainly heralded the end of a conflict that had dominated world politics for 45 years. However, in 1989 the Soviet Union still existed. It would survive until its eventual disintegration in 1991.

Conclusion

By 1990, events were running out of control for Gorbachev. He had started out wanting to reform communism, but he could not control the forces that he had released. The Soviet Union was breaking up as its various republics declared independence. The Baltic states of Latvia, Lithuania and Estonia were relatively late additions to the Soviet Union. During 1990, all declared their independence from Moscow rule.

Within Russia there were demonstrations for change and Boris Yeltsin was elected as leader of the Russian Republic. 'Old fashioned' pro-communists within Russia tried to turn the clock back with an attempted seizure of power in 1991 but this failed in the face of widespread resistance, led by Boris Yeltsin, alongside the refusal of Gorbachev to give into their demands.

The end of the Soviet Union was now inevitable, but even up to the end the ghosts of the Cold War continued to haunt the world. In 1991, the Soviet Union and United States signed up to massive reductions in their nuclear arsenals with the Strategic Arms Reduction Treaty.

The Cold War ended with the USA as the last man standing. On 25 December 1991 the Soviet Union ceased to exist when it was dissolved by its member republics. The Red flag that flew above the Kremlin in Moscow was lowered.

Interpretation and argument

There is considerable historical disagreement about why the Cold War ended. On one side are those who see Ronald Reagan as important. His firm anti-communist stance, increase in military spending and, crucially, the development of the idea that the Cold War could be militarily won put pressure on the Soviets and directly led to the collapse of communism. Writers like J. Gaddis follow this line of thinking. Other historians think that this is not true as there was no resultant increase in Soviet military expenditure once the Strategic Defence Initiative was announced, plus SDI was simply not a credible threat. The argument continues that it was not military spending by America that caused the end of the Cold War, but rather the political realisation by a new political leader in the Soviet Union, Gorbachev, that the current situation in international relations could not continue. Engagement with the West and reform of communism were the way ahead. Historians like R. Gathoff follow this line of thinking. Indeed, the former US Secretary of State James Baker supports the view that the end of the Cold War would not have begun but for Gorbachev. This new political thinking by Gorbachev led to the release of forces that were not controllable and would lead to the collapse of communism.

Rafael Reuveny and Aseem Prakash have argued that the role of Afghanistan in ending the Cold War is neglected. The failure of the Soviet

military in Afghanistan discredited the military, encouraged criticism and paved the way for glasnost and perestroika.

What was the legacy of the Cold War?

The Cold War did not result in a nuclear war, but there were many other conflicts around the world linked to the ideological struggle between communism and capitalism that led to the loss of millions of lives. Korea, Vietnam and Afghanistan are three that we have looked at in this book.

The legacy of the Cold War can be seen in the massive use of resources to produce nuclear weapons. The reduction in armaments and clean up afterwards costs the world even today.

The ending of the Cold War has also unleashed new problems for the world. Communism kept a lid on many conflicts in Eastern Europe and the Middle East. For example, the ending of communist control in Yugoslavia in the 1990s unleashed ethnic conflict between Serbs, Croats and Muslims.

It can be argued that the origins of militant Islam also lie in the Cold War. The Americans armed the Mujahideen in Afghanistan to fight communism. Among the Mujahideen were the Taliban.

Activities

In fours:

- One person take the topic 'Afghanistan and the end of the Cold War'.
- One person take the topic 'Ronald Reagan and the end of the Cold War'.
- One person take the topic 'Mikhail Gorbachev and the end of the Cold War'.
- One person take the topic 'Poland and the end of the Cold War'.

Read this chapter and make a note of all the reasons why the Cold War ended that are relevant for your topic. You will need to find at least ten facts/reasons for each topic.

You now have to teach your fellow group members your topic.

You will have to decide how to make the topic interesting for your partner. You might use a number of ways to do this. Do not just provide a list of notes.

You might:

- make up a quiz
- create a large wordsearch with clues
- draw a spider diagram
- produce a presentation using visuals/pictures for each of the effects you have identified.

Above all be creative. As a group, decide on success criteria for your lesson before you start your research.

Unit assessment practice

Complete a unit assessment standard:

> European and World Outcome 2 asks you to draw on and apply knowledge and understanding of complex European and World historical issues in a number of ways.

> Assessment standard 2.3 asks you to analyse a European and World historical issue.

An example might be:

Analyse the factors which were important in causing the end of the Cold War.

Extended response practice and Top Tip 6: How to write a good conclusion

This top tip provides advice on how to write a good conclusion. The first thing to remember is that your essay or extended response **must** have a conclusion. For your extended response (essay) there are 4 available marks for structure. You can gain 2 out of these 4 marks for your conclusion. Don't dismiss 2 marks as unimportant. 2 marks is the difference between a lower grade and a higher one and the 4 marks for structure could be the difference between a band C and a band A.

The examples provided here all relate to the topic of this section which is: 'An evaluation of the reasons for the end of the Cold War.'

What sort of question will I be asked?

When you are preparing for the exam think very carefully about the style of question you will be asked and what the question will be about. In this case **all** the extended response questions will be about the issue mentioned above. In simple English, the issue means – why did the Cold War end?

In this section you are asked to evaluate – or judge – the reasons why the Cold War ended. Just as in the previous sections, the SQA provides illustrative examples of reasons to use in this section. In this case, the reasons provided as explanations of why the Cold War ended are:

- the defeat of the Soviet Union in Afghanistan
- the failure of communism in Eastern Europe
- soviet economic weakness
- the role of Gorbachev
- western economic strength
- the role of Reagan.

There is no one correct answer which explains why the Cold War ended, so a marker is looking for you to explain all the possible reasons and then prioritise them by deciding which of the reasons you think were more or less important than the others in causing the end of the Cold War. The important thing to do is make sure you have explained all the causes suggested within the illustrative areas for this topic before you make your final decision in response to the question. And don't forget to include your reasons for your choice!

Possible questions on Topic 6 are:

1 To what extent did the defeat of the Soviet Union in Afghanistan make the end of the Cold War inevitable?

2 'The role of President Reagan was the most important reason for the end of the Cold War.' How valid is this view?

3 How important were the relative economic strengths of the West and the Soviet Union in bringing the Cold War to a close?

Now start planning your extended response and the first thing to remember is that your essay **must** have a conclusion. If you do not end with a clearly indicated conclusion you will lose 2 marks. That is a whole results band you would throw away! Your conclusion must do certain things to get the 2 marks and it is not enough just to write a summary of points you have already made. The SQA has stated that a good conclusion should be balanced, it should summarise the arguments and it should come to an overall judgement directly related to the question. That is quite a lot to think about when you head towards the end of your extended response and time is likely to be running out so this top tip is to provide an effective model for a conclusion that can be used in **any** extended response.

Here is the model for your concluding paragraph:

Sentence/part 1 – 'In conclusion …' – indicates the conclusion has started. You should suggest there are different points of view about the main idea contained in the question.

Sentence/part 2 – 'On one hand …' – provides a summary of some points that take one view of the question.

Sentence/part 3 – 'On the other hand …' – completes the summary by summing up the different views and this provides the balance.

Sentence/part 4 – 'Overall …' – provides a final answer to the main question, which means you make a decision. You might decide that one idea was more important than the others and that means you are prioritising.

Now apply this to a question such as:

'The role of President Reagan was the most important reason for the end of the Cold War. How valid is this view?'

In conclusion, the role of Ronald Reagan was important in bringing the Cold War to an end when it did.

On one hand, Reagan brought an aggressive anti-communism to Cold War relations. In 1983 he denounced the Soviet Union as an 'evil empire' and he actively sought to challenge Soviet weakness and strengthen the West in order to defeat communism.

On the other hand, there were other reasons for the end of the Cold War such as the role of Mikhail Gorbachev who saw that the USSR could not afford a new arms race. The Soviet economy was at breaking point. Gorbachev implemented policies of Perestroika and Glasnost which aimed to reform the Soviet economy and liberalise its political system. In so doing, Gorbachev was instrumental in ending the Cold War.

Overall, Reagan was very important to ending the Cold War. Were it not for Reagan's determination to outspend the USSR in terms of the arms race and put further pressure on the Soviet regime, then the Cold War would not have ended when it did.

It is important that you practice this style of conclusion so you can produce it under time pressure and without too much hard thinking. After all, it does what you are asked to do. It is balanced, summarises the arguments and it makes an overall judgement, so it should get 2 marks guaranteed.

Another possible question on Section 6 of the Cold War topic is:

'Mikhail Gorbachev's policies were the most important reason for the end of the Cold War. How valid is this view?'

References

For all photographs please see page ii.

Chapter 1

Sir Winston Churchill (1946) 'The Sinews of Peace' speech quoted from Robert Rhodes James (ed.), *Winston S. Churchill: His Complete Speeches 1897–1963*, Volume VII: 1943–1949, New York: Chelsea House Publishers 1974, 7285–7293 (p. 11)

Harry S. Truman (12 March 1947) *Address of the President to Congress, Recommending Assistance to Greece and Turkey.* Document 171; 80th Congress, 1st Session; Records of the United States House of Representatives; Record Group 233; National Archives (p. 12)

Chapter 2

'Working Notes from the Session of the CPSU CC Presidium on 31 October 1956' October 31, 1956, History and Public Policy Program Digital Archive, TsKhSD, F. 3, Op. 12, D. 1006, Ll. 15–18ob, compiled by V. N. Malin. Translated for CWIHP by Mark Kramer. http://digitalarchive.wilsoncenter.org/document/117064 (p. 33)

Resolution adopted at plenary meeting of the Building Industry Technology University (22 October 1956), from *Report of the Special Committee on the Problem of Hungary, UN General Assembly*, p.69 Official Records: Eleventh Session, Supplement No. 18 (A/3592) (p. 39)

Chapter 3

Nikita Sergeyevich Khrushchev (1970) *Khrushchev Remembers*, Boston: Little Brown & Company (pp. 47–48)

Chapter 4

Dwight D. Eisenhower 'The President's News Conference of April 7, 1954' from *Public Papers of the Presidents*, 1954, p. 383 (p. 61)

Michael Bilton & Kevin Sim (1992) *Four Hours in My Lai*, New York: Penguin, p. 335 (p. 67)

Index